Convergent Journalism: An Introduction

"Convergent Journalism: An Introduction" is a pioneering textbook that will teach you how to master the skills needed to be a journalist in today's converged media landscape. This book shows you what makes a news story effective, and how to identify the best platform for a particular story, whether it's the Web, broadcast or print. The bedrock tenets of journalism remain at the core of this book, including information dissemination, storytelling and audience engagement. After establishing these journalism basics, the book goes into great detail on how to tailor a story to meet the needs of various media.

Vincent F. Filak has brought this second edition completely up to date through:

- A thorough reorganization of the chapters, which provides a newer, more practical approach focused on 'how to do convergent journalism,' rather than simply observing the current state of converged media.
- A number of new pedagogical features to improve learning and retention, including examples, exercises, breakout boxes and more.
- Coverage of additional topics such as issues of law and ethics in digital media, and also writing for mobile platforms and social media.
- A companion website with links to additional exam~~~ ~~~~~~ text, images and multimedia for students, as well a~ site with a test bank, suggested exercises and discuss

Vincent F. Filak, Ph.D. is an associate professor at the Wisconsin Oshkosh, where he teaches writing and editing courses and serves as the adviser to the school's award-winning newspaper,

The Advance-Titan. He has taught journalism courses at the University of Missouri, the University of Wisconsin and Ball State University, where he also advised the Ball State Daily News. He produced the first edition of this book, "Convergent Journalism: An Introduction," with Dr. Stephen Quinn, and co-authored the book "The Journalist's Handbook for Online Editing" with Dr. Kenneth L. Rosenauer. He has contributed to the books "Media in an American Crisis: Studies of Sept. 11, 2001" and "Understanding Media Convergence," and has extensively published research on issues of media convergence, e-learning and student journalism.

Convergent Journalism: An Introduction

Writing and Producing across Media

2nd Edition

Edited by
Vincent F. Filak

First published 2005 by Focal Press

This edition published 2015 by Focal Press
70 Blanchard Road, Suite 402, Burlington, MA 01803

and by Focal Press
2 Park Square, Milton Park, Abingdon, Oxon OX14 4RN

Focal Press is an imprint of the Taylor & Francis Group, an informa business

© 2015 Taylor & Francis

The right of the editor to be identified as the author of the editorial material, and of the authors for their individual chapters, has been asserted in accordance with sections 77 and 78 of the Copyright, Designs and Patents Act 1988.

All rights reserved. No part of this book may be reprinted or reproduced or utilised in any form or by any electronic, mechanical, or other means, now known or hereafter invented, including photocopying and recording, or in any information storage or retrieval system, without permission in writing from the publishers.

Notices
Knowledge and best practice in this field are constantly changing. As new research and experience broaden our understanding, changes in research methods, professional practices, or medical treatment may become necessary.

Practitioners and researchers must always rely on their own experience and knowledge in evaluating and using any information, methods, compounds, or experiments described herein. In using such information or methods they should be mindful of their own safety and the safety of others, including parties for whom they have a professional responsibility.

Product or corporate names may be trademarks or registered trademarks, and are used only for identification and explanation without intent to infringe.

Library of Congress Cataloging in Publication Data
Convergent journalism: an introduction writing and producing across media /
    edited by Vincent F. Filak. — Second edition.
    pages cm.
    1. Online journalism. 2. Broadcast journalism. 3. Mass media—Ownership.
    4. Convergence (Telecommunication) I. Filak, Vincent F., editor.
    PN4784.O62C66 2015
    070.4—dc23
    2014024248

ISBN: 978-1-138-77505-3 (pbk)
ISBN: 978-1-138-77500-8 (hbk)
ISBN: 978-1-315-77349-0 (ebk)

Typeset in Berling and Futura
by Florence Production Ltd, Stoodleigh, Devon, UK

To Amy and Zoe, the loves of my life.
And to mom and dad, who never let me
quit on anything.

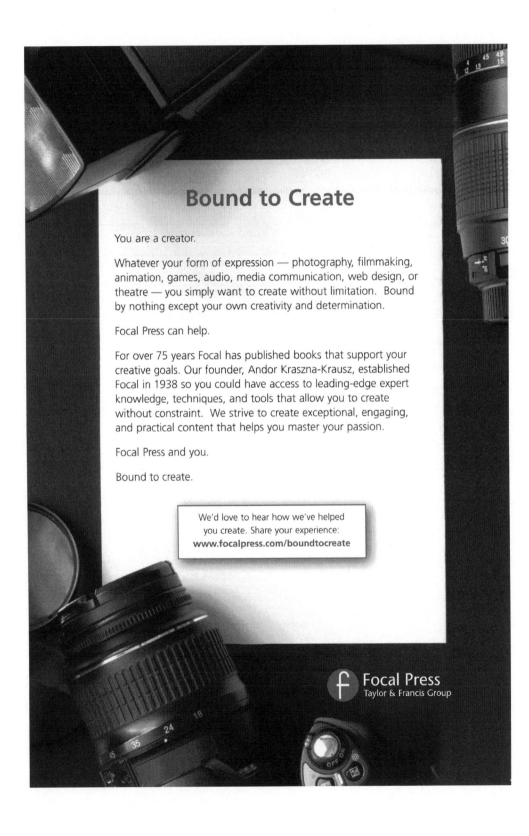

Bound to Create

You are a creator.

Whatever your form of expression — photography, filmmaking, animation, games, audio, media communication, web design, or theatre — you simply want to create without limitation. Bound by nothing except your own creativity and determination.

Focal Press can help.

For over 75 years Focal has published books that support your creative goals. Our founder, Andor Kraszna-Krausz, established Focal in 1938 so you could have access to leading-edge expert knowledge, techniques, and tools that allow you to create without constraint. We strive to create exceptional, engaging, and practical content that helps you master your passion.

Focal Press and you.

Bound to create.

We'd love to hear how we've helped
you create. Share your experience:
www.focalpress.com/boundtocreate

Focal Press
Taylor & Francis Group

Contents

viii

7 Information Graphics   101

Jennifer George-Palilonis, Professor,
Ball State University

8 Audio and Video Journalism   121

Erika Engstrom, Professor and
Gary Larson, Associate Professor-in-Residence,
University of Nevada, Las Vegas

xi

9 Data-driven Journalism 141

Bob Britten, Assistant Professor,
West Virginia University

12 The Law and Convergent Journalism   201

Daxton R. "Chip" Stewart, Associate Professor
and Associate Dean, Texas Christian University

13 Ethics in the Digital Age   219

Tracy Everbach, Associate Professor,
University of North Texas

xiii

Acknowledgments

This book would not have been possible without the time, talent and skills of a group of authors I have lovingly dubbed "the smartest people I know." Thanks to Glenn Hubbard, Scott Reinardy, Tim Gleason, Jennifer George-Palilonis, Erika Engstrom, Gary Larson, Bob Britten, Sara Steffes Hansen, Steve Chappell, Chip Stewart and Tracy Everbach for your willingness to participate in this project and your ability to get this job done. This text is special in how it touches on many areas of journalism. Your unique talents have made it a book that bridges the gap between education and practice as well as traditional journalism and digital media.

I am also grateful to Stephen Quinn, my coauthor on the first edition of this book, who allowed me to see the possibilities for a text like this one. In addition, I am extremely grateful to Natasha Soglin for her incredible vision and artistic talent that helped make the cover of this book absolutely amazing.

A special thanks goes out to the crew at Focal Press, including the reviewers of our work and those involved in making sure this book was everything it could be. I would especially like to thank Kathryn Morrissey, who was willing to take a chance on a second edition almost a decade after the first edition was published. The faith you had that this could be something worthwhile drove each and every one of us to work harder and do better than we thought was possible. Thanks, Katy.

Defining Convergence

Vincent F. Filak

Introduction

Looking back on the previous edition of this book is a lot like looking at old photos of fashion models – some things look great in retrospect while others look ridiculous. In the early 2000s, this book set out to define what journalism was becoming as well as how best to prepare students for this new and changing world. In some cases, our predictions were right on the money. In other cases, we would have been better off telling you that you could have a flying car soon.

Newspaper journalism's decline was a prominent concern for us when we started our look at convergent journalism. We saw some incremental growth of cross-platform cooperation among print and broadcast journalists throughout the United States. Portable phones had not emerged as information-gathering tools, but were primarily used for person-to-person communication. Mobile devices, such as tablets and smartphones, that operated on ever-present Wi-Fi signals were years away from becoming dominant players in the media landscape.

The one thing from the previous edition that remains a crucial part of journalism is the importance of learning a broad array of skills. Journalists will always need many storytelling tools and this book will help you learn what they are and how to effectively use them. Regardless of the platform you use, journalism remains about sharing information, engaging audience members and telling stories. Those values remain a focal point of this book.

This introductory chapter will define convergent journalism, discuss why it remains important in the field of media and explain how journalists can thrive in a convergent media environment.

Convergence Defined

When we first published this book in 2005, the term "convergence" was a buzzword on the lips of most people in the media industry. To some people, it was a way to get TV and print journalists to work with one another. To others, it was a business move geared toward mergers of corporate interests that would allow for certain news conglomerates to own a larger share of the media pie. To some cynics, it was a scam that would allow companies to force fewer journalists to do more work, thus creating fewer jobs and worse journalism.

In reviewing the changes in the field to date, it is possible that all of those views have some merit. However, as far as this book is concerned, we are viewing convergence as an attempt to draw from the strengths of various media platforms in order to better tell stories. The goal of convergence is to provide audience members with content they need, in formats they like, in a way they will accept.

Convergence in Education

Various large, public universities have relied on a convergent approach to create journalists for this millennium. The University of Missouri, for example, notes in its convergence curriculum, "The public increasingly wants to access quality news and information at any time through any and all media that are convenient or appealing to them." To this end, students at that university are trained to be storytellers, with the idea that they will master at least one platform and use the others to augment their work.

Syracuse University hosts a convergence lab that allows students to work across media platforms and, as of 2014, was completing an $18 million project that comprehensively upgrades the school's news production studio. The University of Kansas' website emphasizes its status as a "leader in media convergence," noting that it has a news/information major for students who want to explore a variety of storytelling options from print through online. Other institutions, including Ball State University, New Mexico State University and Auburn University, have also made heavy financial commitments to this model of teaching skills across platforms.

Private and smaller schools have also invested in this approach to teaching journalism. Lynchburg College, located in Virginia, allows students to study convergent journalism as part of a major or a minor in communication studies. The school notes that students there will study traditional textual, audio and video storytelling while engaging in work that appeals to an interactive global community. Students will broaden their "understanding of audience needs, the media industry and the social impact of communication methods." Other institutions, such as Oral Roberts University, Indiana Wesleyan and Delaware State University, also offer programs that emphasize storytelling across platforms as the key component of convergence education.

On the international stage, schools around the globe have offered convergence education. The University of Kent, which is frequently ranked among the top 30 British universities, offers courses on the principles and practices of convergent journalism. Students there compile traditional news packages and also produce work specifically for an Internet audience. The University of Derby in England also offers courses in multi-platform and convergent journalism, with an emphasis on serving the needs of audience members. Shantou University and Nanjing University in China and Moscow State University in Russia are just a few of the other educational institutions that have established a convergent journalism curriculum.

Despite the wide array of educational approaches at these institutions, we have embraced two focal points for defining convergence and making it work effectively – quality information gathering and effective storytelling. The core of journalism remains about getting information from one group of people and then translating it into a usable format for other people to consume. These elements have not changed and probably never will. What has changed is the ways in which people consume the media, how much time they spend with it and how best to go about reaching them with the content we have gathered and want to share.

Why Convergence Matters

Whether people call it "multi-platform journalism," "multimedia journalism," "digital journalism" or "convergence," the idea that people want information wherever and whenever they see fit is at the center of this approach to media. Journalists who were once asked to do one

3

thing particularly well, such as write stories or shoot photos, are now asked to do many things extremely well. Even journalists who are allowed to specialize in one form of storytelling are required to do more with their work for multiple platforms.

Below is a list of items that will explain why working across platforms in a converged environment has value:

Ever-increasing media usage

In the first edition of this book, we noted that consumers spent a large portion of each day using media. The book cited the 2004 Communication Industry Forecast, which stated that the average consumer spent 3,663 hours with media in 2003, or approximately 10 hours per day. The forecast's experts at Veronis Suhler Stevenson (VSS) now predict that people spend about 3,706 hours per year with media, or almost 12 minutes more per day. They also predict that that number will grow to 3,805 hours by 2016.

In addition, how people get their information has significantly changed as well. In the mid 2000s, cellular telephones were primarily a source of person-to-person communication, with audio and texting capabilities. However, as the decade progressed, technological leaps allowed for phones to do more than send and receive individual messages. Devices like the iPhone, which launched in 2007, allowed individuals to surf the Web, play games and download content. The telephone became more of a mini-computer with multimedia capabilities, thus allowing users to get information anywhere, from many outlets.

As people continue to get more information from a variety of sources, they will reshape their media habits in ways that best serve their interests. As your audience continues to expand its media use, you can employ the multi-platform approach of convergence to satisfy their needs.

Audience demands

Journalism used to be about what journalists wrote and what readers consumed. The New York Times' boastful tag line of "All the News That's Fit to Print" has a sense that the journalists know what matters most and the audience should be grateful to receive this important information. However, with a shift to digital media and the explosion of channels available to people, audience members will continue to have more and more choices in what they consume.

Cory Haik, the executive producer and senior editor for digital news at The Washington Post, wrote that journalists' biggest job now is to deliver good journalism for people on a variety of devices. In her essay for the Nieman Journalism Lab, she noted that news must "be exactly there for people no matter what they're doing or where they're doing it." She called this approach "adaptive journalism" and it incorporates innovations in editorial content, user behavior, technology and even advertising to deliver messages in a way that the audience craves.

News organizations, however, seem unaware of or unwilling to embrace the public's role in determining what matters most. Pablo Boczkowski, the director of the program in Media, Technology and Society at Northwestern University, notes that a gap of almost 20 percentage points exists between what journalists highlight as being important and what users click on the most. Boczkowski notes that although news organizations might start paying more attention to audience desires, journalists must be careful not to shovel "junk food" at the audience members just to satisfy their desires.

Convergence efforts run the risk of pandering to audience whims instead of serving audience needs. The difference may seem insignificant, but the more journalists blur the line between these concepts, the worse it can be for the audience. When you serve your audience members, you find information that matters to them (see Chapter 3 for more on this) and you present it to them on platforms and with media that best fit their lives. An example of this could be the coverage of a traffic crash on a major highway near rush hour. You would immediately use Twitter to get the basic information out to people who follow your news outlet. If you have access to a radio platform, you would then announce the information there as well. This approach helps people driving home get what they need in a way that will help them avoid the problematic spot on the freeway. You can then use a Web, video or print story to augment your coverage and fill in details about the cause, damage and reason behind the crash. People who are interested can read this after they have avoided the disaster on the ride home.

Pandering is where journalists look more at what "sells" and less at what matters. Instead of presenting important news, journalists can find themselves promoting videos of cats flushing toilets or waterskiing squirrels to keep page views high and advertisers happy. Other less-ethical practices promise things in the headline or the link that the story can't help to deliver. This approach is often derided as "click

5

bait" and will diminish the likelihood that consumers will continue to trust you or go to you for content. However, media organizations have always risked allowing sensationalism to overtake quality in the quest for readership and viewership. As Haik points out, the key to making journalism work in the digital environment is to give consumers things they need where and when they need them. This is both an old maxim and a current requirement for journalists.

Time is of the essence

Journalists always pride themselves on getting the freshest information out to the public faster than the competition. TV stations could take several bites at the news apple with their afternoon, evening and nightly newscasts while daily newspapers often relied on either one or two editions per news cycle to inform the public. Weekly papers, monthly magazines and other less frequent publications used news features or deeper thought pieces to help readers make sense of bigger issues.

The number of outlets available for media users has exponentially increased in the past decade or so, and many of these outlets cover news faster and better than their traditional counterparts. Websites, Twitter feeds, Facebook news feeds and other digital media can run circles around traditional media. These changes in how timeliness is measured have led print and broadcast operations to embrace digital technologies and evolving media platforms. The skill sets associated with traditional media, such as writing and videography, remain valuable on the traditional platforms but also translate well in a fast-paced environment in which news and information are constantly evolving.

Self-interest

If none of these arguments are persuasive to you, consider the most basic argument of all: Convergence skills will make you employable. If you examine publications such as Editor & Publisher or surf journalism employment sites such as journalismjobs.com, you will see job postings that require you to do all (or most) of the things outlined in this book. You cannot assume that you will be able to write for just one medium or be good at just one thing. In Chapter 11, we discuss what it takes to get a job in this multimedia, converged world and even outline a position description that shows you we are a long way from the days of the "print or broadcast" dichotomy.

How to "Do" Convergence

The challenge of performing journalistic tasks in a converged environment can seem daunting or even impossible. The best way to avoid becoming overwhelmed is to focus on a few basic journalistic themes. In each chapter, the following thematic threads will help you see how to apply each tool properly as part of a convergent journalistic effort.

The consumer comes first

Newer journalists often make the mistake of working for themselves, their sources or their media outlet. Even seasoned journalists can fall into the trap of producing content that serves their own needs first. The problem with this approach is that it fails to keep the focus on the people who matter most – the consumers.

With all of the available options people have for getting information, journalists need to think of themselves as being more beholden to the audience than they did in years past. When only one or two newspapers and three or four TV stations served an area, people were stuck with whatever they got. If they were dissatisfied, they could write a letter to the editor or call the news station, but that was about it. Now, people can turn to 100 or more channels of news and millions of digital outlets, each of which can provide them with the information they want.

Journalists should not ignore the core values of journalism when they work to serve the consumers, but they should look at their work through a different lens. These core values include accuracy, clarity, focus, value and more. In addition, journalists should still rely on the news values of timeliness, impact, conflict, prominence and more when determining news content. Just because the audience members might love watching videos of waterskiing hamsters or reading lists like "31 ways you are like Lady Gaga," it doesn't follow that journalists should produce content like this.

However, journalists need to see how they can use their content to engage consumers as opposed to just producing content in the easiest available way. This means telling the story in the most complete way possible. It also means spending time to explain difficult concepts and complicated issues. The journalists also need to communicate in a way that consumers can embrace. They shouldn't write whatever comes out of a source's mouth and assume the audience members will figure it out somehow.

Right tool, right job

Philosophers and psychologists have often spoken of the "Law of the Instrument," which has been boiled down to the phrase, "If all you have is a hammer, everything looks like a nail." The idea is that people tend to rely too much on a familiar tool and this approach can cause problems when it comes to convergent journalism.

Journalists were traditionally taught in "silos," where they were given a specific tool, such as a video camera or a pen and notebook, and told how to use it as part of their job. Journalists got very little insight regarding how to work across media platforms. Therefore, when they now receive a variety of tools, ranging from photos and graphics through audio and video, journalists tend to panic. They then cling to the most familiar tool and use it regardless of its applicability to the task at hand.

In convergence, you need to learn the benefits and drawbacks of each tool. Video can be a great storytelling tool in some cases and a lousy one in others. For example, a story on a symphony's efforts to bring Mozart to children would be great as a video or audio story. It would be less valuable in print, as it would lose the audio aspects that make the story worth telling.

Graphics can make a story much easier to understand or they can create a convoluted mess. An example of this is how a timeline can lay out an extended court trial or a long-term project. However, a graphic that shows a wide view of a state with only three small dots on it, all around a single city, is visually pointless. The idea is that each tool has strengths and weaknesses and a big part of your job is to find the right tool and use it in the right situation. When you do this, you serve your audience well.

Tell stories

Each tool we explore in this book can help you tell stories. Storytelling happens when you capture a sliver of time with a still-frame image, outline a complex procedure with a compelling graphic or write text that paints a picture in the mind's eye. Storytelling is also the best way to engage your audience. People love stories because stories turn complicated concepts into relatable ideas. Stories also help people remember important things while they enjoy the underlying tale the journalist weaves.

In many cases, the desire to gather quotes or images overtakes the journalist and the storytelling gets lost. Instead of just finding the components that will complete a story or finish a video package, you should focus on the concept of telling stories. Think about what people most want to know and then tell them a story that gets them that information. This approach will work well across all the tools and with all media users.

Final Thoughts

This chapter is meant to set the stage for the remainder of the book. What comes next will be a hands-on experience in which you will learn what to do and how to do it in a convergent environment. The intention of this approach is to help you see not only how to create this form of journalism, but also why you should approach things in certain ways.

In compiling this book, the goal was simple: Figure out what things matter most in journalism, find really smart people in each of these areas and let those people tell you everything they think you should know. These authors are educators with strong professional backgrounds and they have blended both the idealistic and the practical aspects of their topics as they share their thoughts with you.

The book will walk you through the aspects of top-notch journalism, starting with writing and reporting for text-based stories and branching into the visual arts of photography, graphics and video journalism. The book will also delve heavily into the digital realm, with chapters on interactivity, social media and multimedia storytelling. In addition, chapters on law and ethics provide you with a wider look at the rules and implications associated with the field journalism.

Throughout these chapters, the authors emphasize the basic-level skills associated with each area while simultaneously weaving in the nuances associated with convergent journalism and digitally based media. The results should be an engaging and useful text that can lead to a well-rounded reader and strong convergent journalist.

Writing Across Platforms

Glenn Hubbard

2

Introduction

"I'm sorry, but this isn't what I want to do. I'm going into print."

I probably heard some variation on that statement dozens of times during the semester Caitlin took my video news production course. I frequently responded that video skills were also important for newspaper reporters in the Internet age. I sometimes uttered a warning to the effect of, "Well, you never know what the future holds." I saw Caitlin after that semester and I was happy to hear she attained the managing editor position at our university's student paper. I was confident she would do well after graduation. Later, I found out I was right about that: She landed a full-time journalism job at a reputable news organization right out of college.

She says her work closely resembles what she did at the student paper – assigning reporters to stories, making editorial decisions, organizing news content and writing. Interestingly enough, Caitlin's first job is at a local television station, working as a producer in charge of evening newscasts. She says she now loves television and hopes to make a career of it.

Caitlin's story is becoming more and more common. Journalism students head down the path of newspapers or television, only to find the skills they learned apply just as easily to other portions of the field.

The lines between print, broadcast and online writing will continue to blur, but the underlying value of effective writing remains at the core of each discipline. Throughout this book, we will emphasize how things have changed in the field and how life will change for you as you move from students to professional journalists. For now, we will primarily focus on the aspect of writing and how what seems to be a radical set of changes in the field is really more of an adjustment in your thinking and your approach to your audience.

A typical media-writing textbook emphasizes differences between text-based (print) and spoken-word (broadcast) writing. Print writing is for the eye; broadcast is for the ear. Print sentences are long and varied; broadcast sentences are consistently short and stick to one structure most of the time. Print sentences are information-rich; broadcasters generally limit themselves to one or two facts per sentence. Print writers have more space for depth; broadcast writers keep things simple.

The differences above are technically correct, but they miss a larger point: Many professionals do both well as they seamlessly switch back and forth between writing for the eye and the ear. Television journalists create Web versions of their stories, often using the same Associated Press style guidelines required of print reporters. Similarly, most newspaper websites include multimedia content, some of which closely resembles television or radio news. This chapter is about writing across platforms, but it's not about two drastically different approaches to writing. It's about having multiple options for how to present information.

This chapter includes tips for mass-media writing that are useful regardless of platform. It will also clarify similarities and differences between print and spoken-word writing that are commonly mis-understood by aspiring media professionals.

What Are You Trying To Say? Well, Write That

The first thing I tell my students about broadcast or spoken-word writing is that it's not writing at all. It's talking. Often, when a student is struggling with how to compose a sentence, I'll ask the person to tell me what he or she is trying to say. "Write that" is my frequent reply. Experienced writers can produce good stories without opening their mouths, but there is an auditory component to the process of writing.

Writing and talking are closely linked because we hear words in our heads as we read. That's why experts on dyslexia and other reading difficulties say some of these issues result from a breakdown between the parts of the brain that process vision and hearing. People who see words and are unable to imagine what they sound like have difficulty understanding what they mean, and a similar logic applies to those with normal reading comprehension. Good writing sounds good in your head, and one of the best ways to hear it in your head is to hear it with your ears. Therefore, it is helpful to say things out loud before typing them.

A useful rule is: "Say it. Write it. Say it again." This approach allows you to talk your thoughts out first to figure out the clearest way to express them. After you have a handle on what you want to say, type up your thoughts and then read aloud what you just typed to make sure it sounds right. It's a good idea to do this on a sentence-by-sentence basis, but it's also a good idea to backtrack frequently to check for overall flow.

A related rule of thumb is not to look at notes, press releases and wire copy while writing. Put those aside where you can't see them and just talk out what you're trying to say. If you don't know the facts well enough to write something, you're not ready to write anyway. Spend more time familiarizing yourself with the facts, put them aside and then write. You can always double-check your notes later to make sure you got the details correct. Like so many concepts we'll cover in this chapter, these tips are equally useful when writing for print, broadcast, the Web and other media platforms.

13

Write for Someone Other Than Yourself

Most of us who chose the journalism profession did so, at least in part, because we had a knack for writing. The main problem is that we either don't know or don't embrace the notion that journalistic writing is for others, not ourselves.

Good writers often have expansive vocabularies and pride themselves on using words that look impressive on the page, regardless of whether they're familiar to regular folks. However, your job is to help people understand information, not show off how smart you are. This usually means following a rule famously expressed by author George Orwell: "Never use a long word when a short one will do." It also means *not* using the right-click thesaurus function in Microsoft Word.

But There Are Some Differences . . . Sort Of

Writing for spoken word is significantly different from print because it's really talking. When you speak to someone about a story you're working on, you probably use shorter, simpler sentences than the information-rich ones you would write in a newspaper article. You probably put the subject first most of the time, because that's how you talk. Very few people say, "Considering that I am hungry and it has been six hours since I last ate, I suggest that we go to lunch." Most just say, "Let's go to lunch. I'm hungry. It's been six hours since I ate anything." That's the difference between "writing" and "talking," and if you think of it that way, you'll have no trouble going back and forth between text and spoken word.

One more analogy: When you give a PowerPoint presentation about a paper you wrote, you don't just read the paper word-for-word (unless you're trying to cure insomnia). You most likely speak in conversational phrases and might even condense bullet points so they are easily digestible. That's like converting a print news story into a spoken-word format – simply "telling" someone about the story, as in the example below:

PRINT STORY

A two-vehicle accident at the intersection of Algoma Boulevard and Wisconsin Avenue caused damage to UW Oshkosh property and three students' parked vehicles Wednesday night.

The accident, which was between a white Honda SUV and a blue Ford Taurus, occurred at approximately 4:24 p.m., according to Oshkosh Police Officer Rob Kraemer of the Crash Investigation Team.

"The white vehicle was going to make a left-hand turn and go down Algoma," Kraemer said. "The blue vehicle was traveling southbound on Wisconsin. The white vehicle turned left in front of that vehicle and they collided. The blue vehicle then went up over the curb and struck the two parked motorcycles, and then one of the motorcycles hit a parked car next to it."

The driver of the Honda, who was not carrying passengers, was charged with "failure to yield to those in the right of way while taking a left-hand turn," according to Kraemer. The driver of the Taurus had one passenger in the vehicle.

No one appeared injured as a result of the accident, but those involved were complaining of aches and pains, according to Kraemer.

Five vehicles total were involved in the accident, three of which were parked in the South Scott Hall parking lot where the Taurus ended up.

A large campus directional sign was hit down by the blue car and was by removed from the scene by Campus Facilities Management. The cost to replace the sign is yet to be determined, according to LeMire.

TELLING THE STORY

You: Hey Joe, did you hear a wreck messed up some UW Oshkosh property and a couple of parked cars yesterday afternoon?

Joe: Really? Where?

You: At the intersection of Algoma Boulevard and Wisconsin Avenue.

Joe: What happened?

You: Well, a white Honda SUV was turning left onto Algoma and hit a blue Ford Taurus at around 4:30.

Joe: How bad was it?

You: Nobody was seriously hurt, but the Taurus got knocked into three parked cars and also hit a campus directional sign.

Joe: Anybody get a ticket?

You: The driver of the Honda was charged with "failure to yield."

Joe: What are they going to do about the messed up sign?

You: The police say they don't know how much it'll cost to replace.

BROADCAST STORY

A wreck damaged some UW Oshkosh property and a couple of parked vehicles yesterday afternoon. It happened at the intersection of Algoma Boulevard and Wisconsin Avenue. Police say a Honda SUV was turning left onto Algoma and hit a Ford Taurus at around 4:30. Nobody was seriously hurt, but the Taurus got knocked into three parked cars and also hit a campus directional sign. The driver of the SUV was charged with "failure to yield." Police say they don't know how much it'll cost to replace the sign.

Note: The above example is for the purpose of illustration and because you might need to convert your own print stories to spoken word, but this does not mean it's OK to convert *other people's* print stories into your own spoken-word versions. That would be stealing.

VIEW FROM A PRO

STEPHEN DUBNER

Stephen Dubner is a former New York Times reporter, a former story editor for New York Times magazine, a best-selling author, a nationally known public radio host, a former commentator for the NFL Network and a successful podcaster. However, he is best known for his collaboration with economist Steven Levitt, which resulted in the nonfiction bestsellers "Freakonomics" and "Superfreakonomics", each of which sold more than 4 million copies.

Figure 2.1
Stephen Dubner.

Although many journalists have feared moving from platform to platform, Dubner said he enjoys the freedom and flexibility it provides.

"It's great to have different media or idioms to work in," Dubner said. "Most people who write have a variety of interests and ideas, and it's nice to have the ability to toggle back and forth between media."

However, in writing his most successful books, Dubner deliberately blurred the lines between conversational spoken-word writing, and print style. He said many people are uncomfortable with what he calls numerical narratives, stories built largely on statistical data.

"The voice that I used is a very conversational voice," he said, "and it's also what I would call a fairly interactive voice – meaning talking to the reader – asking the reader, 'Here, I'm going to tell you something; I want you to think about it; and now think about how you think it went; and now I'll tell you how it went.' It's a level of engagement that I thought was necessary."

Dubner said he literally used his own voice to achieve a conversational voice with "Freakonomics".

"Everything I write, when I rewrite, and proof, and edit, I always read out loud," he said. "I really believe in that. I never forget that writing was invented as a means to record conversation – spoken language. That was its primary function, and I think there's still a lot to be said for that."

Despite his successful career as a print journalist, Dubner said he is not a fan of certain approaches to newspaper writing.

"My least favorite writing is the writing that sounds like no one in their right mind would ever speak it aloud," he said. "I understand the need for that sometimes, especially with technical and academic writing, but the New York Times, which I love – I read the leads of the A-1 news stories every day, and what kind of bad computer translation software rendered this from the Croatian into English? Nobody in their right mind speaks like that."

Dubner said he embraced convergence long before the term entered common usage. He has routinely crossed platforms since his college years at Appalachian State University.

"I was actually a broadcast journalism major at Appalachian," he said. "I'd always been a writer, and my dad was a newspaperman, and we had a family newspaper, and I wrote for the college newspaper, but I actually did go there as a broadcast journalism major."

Like many media professionals, Dubner said the Web and social media bring exciting possibilities for aspiring journalists.

"An individual can create his or her own media channel," he said. "You can take an idea and put it into three different formats, you can take three different ideas and put them into one – whatever you want it to be – and I think that's a remarkable opportunity."

Dubner said there are hopeful signs for the economics of the media business.

"I happen to love the public radio model," he said. "I really like that it's essentially funded by voluntary contributions. We've written a little bit about pay-what-you-want schemes generally, and how they work or can work or sometimes fail. That's not a bad model."

Digital and entrepreneurial journalism provide good opportunities, but Dubner said it's still worthwhile to start one's career at an established media outlet if possible.

"If you're an individual starting out in journalism trying to go from zero to something, believe me, I acknowledge it's really hard, so I think it's good to hook yourself to an institution if you can – if only to develop your own self as a brand as you go," he said.

Writing Guidelines

The next section will explore traditional writing style guidelines of broadcasting and print. While it is necessary to use a comparison/contrast format for clarity of explanations, the intent is to demystify the differences.

Sentences, words and phrasing

The same
Use the simplest words and the simplest sentence structures to express a thought. Put the subject as close as possible to the beginning of the sentence, followed as soon as possible by the verb and then the rest of the predicate.

Clarity is the key to all good writing. If a reader is confused, a writer has failed to communicate effectively. If you don't understand something, you can't expect your reader or viewer to understand it. If you don't understand it, either figure it out or leave it out. Achieve clarity first, then think about the fancy stuff.

One of the best ways to attain clarity is through the use of active voice. This requires you to position the words in your sentence in a noun-verb-object format. For example, the simple sentence "Bill hit Bob" is in active voice. The noun is the simple subject (Bill), the verb is the word of action (hit) and the object is the word that receives the action of the verb (Bob). In other words, you are answering the question "Who did what to whom?" and doing so in that order.

Passive voice is the opposite of active voice. It leads to longer sentences with less active verbs (often called linking verbs) and it reverses the order of the pieces. "Bill was hit by Bob" is an example of a passive-voice sentence. As you can see it's longer (five words versus three words), contains a linking verb (was) and is more complicated in terms of order. (For more on this, you can consult any decent grammar textbook or various grammar-based websites.)

Active voice is better than passive, but sometimes passive is acceptable. "Former Israeli Prime Minister Ariel Sharon was laid to rest" is OK because writing that "Israelis laid former prime minister Ariel Sharon to rest" offers little additional information and de-emphasizes Sharon's prominence. More commonly, though, an active sentence such as "A man died" is stronger and more efficient than "A man was killed." That's why media writing instructors emphasize the use of active voice.

Avoid repeated words and phrases. One of the most difficult situations for news writers comes with fire coverage, because these stories can be impossible to write without using the word "fire" repeatedly. For example, a paragraph in a fire story could say, "Firefighters brought the fire under control after 30 minutes, according to Fire Chief John Jones. It was the third fire in the neighborhood this week." Some alternate the word "blaze" with "fire" to reduce repetition, but this raises a question about common usage. There are no easy answers, but crafty use of the pronoun "it" can help, as can selective removal of the word fire when possible, as in "Chief John Jones" instead of "Fire Chief John Jones."

Steer clear of "newsy" words that are also vague, such as alleged, allegedly, reportedly, apparently, officials, authorities and residents. These words are not always wrong but are best used sparingly. Consider how regular people would say something, because that's the best way to make sure they'll understand. Also, keep in mind that the word "allegedly" does *not* protect you from a libel suit. The best rule of thumb is good-old attribution.

Similar

Broadcast: If the thought is too complicated, break it into multiple sentences.

Print: Generally one major fact per sentence (paragraph), but related facts (supporting details) can be worked in as additional clauses or phrases.

Different

Broadcast: Keep sentences short so they can be spoken in one breath, the speaker can easily inflect properly and the listener can easily comprehend. This sometimes means leaving out certain details you might include in a print story. For instance, in spoken-word writing you will generally avoid dependent clauses and appositive phrases because they're hard to say out loud and hard for the listener to follow.

19

Here are a few examples of problematic sentences and a few ways to fix them:

Poor: Archie Jones, 22, assistant director of the American Society of Fraternities and Sororities, says the result is unacceptable. (Long appositive phrase)

Poor: Archie Jones, who is assistant director of the American Society of Fraternities and Sororities, says the result is unacceptable. (Dependent clause)

Better: 22-year-old Archie Jones is assistant director of the American Society of Fraternities and Sororities. He says the result is unacceptable.

Another idea – leave out a few more details: Archie Jones is assistant director of a Greek organization. He says the result is unacceptable.

If this bothers your hardcore print news reporter sensibilities, it's OK, because you can include the additional details in the text version of your story or in a graphic at the bottom of the TV screen.

The operating principle here is that sentences are generally easier to follow when the subject and verb are close together and the total word count is short. This is a key concept in spoken-word writing.

Longer, information-rich sentences are OK in print because the readers can navigate the information at their own pace, but this does not mean all print sentences have to be long and complicated.

Verb tense

The same
If it happened in the past, it is fine to write it that way. The same rule applies with the present and future tenses.

Similar
Broadcasters like to emphasize immediacy because newscasts generally air live. Newspaper stories traditionally favored past tense because writers knew their readers wouldn't see the stories until the next day. This is changing somewhat with the Web and social media, but the important point is that both print and broadcast news writing value timeliness.

Broadcasters sometimes use the present-perfect tense in leads when reporting past occurrences that are relatively new at the time a newscast airs. For example: "Police have made an arrest in connection with a bank robbery that happened yesterday." This is not common in print editions of newspapers but could be useful in tweets or Web stories.

Different
Broadcasters frequently use the simple present tense for story leads: "A man is shot this afternoon." Many TV news producers, and even some writing instructors, consider this acceptable, but the best, most successful writers avoid the practice most of the time. Some may like it for stylistic reasons, but it is a violation of the principle that broadcast writing should be conversational. You wouldn't say to your mom, "I wreck my car this morning," so talking to your television viewer that way makes little sense. If you're looking for a simple rule, here it is: Write for the spoken word the way people talk.

Style

The same
Print and broadcast journalism are stylistically different for reasons discussed previously, but they do have commonalities. News writers should avoid the use of opinionated descriptors. To say "A car ran

into a building" is hardly disputable factually, but as soon as you add that it was a "pretty car" that ran into a "big building," you jeopardize your credibility, because your reader or viewer may disagree. This leads to another stylistic similarity, which is the use of attribution. You could say, "A car witnesses described as pretty ran into a large building, according to an officer at the scene." This detaches your opinion from the story, which is what both print and broadcast news writers do most of the time.

Similar

Broadcast: Use contractions in almost every case where they're possible, because that's the way people talk. The exception is when you're emphasizing the word "not." It's possible to mishear "weren't" or "can't" as "were" or "can," so in such cases it's preferable to say "were not" or "cannot." Most other exceptions result from the personal preferences of certain reporters, producers, anchors or news directors who find contractions too informal.

Print: Traditionally, print journalists avoided contractions, but AP style and many newspapers have loosened this rule in recent years. Ask your instructor or your boss what the preference is, and follow it.

Different

Perhaps the most obvious style difference between print and broadcast journalism results from broadcasters' emphasis on relating to their audiences. Traditional journalistic ethics encourage the reporter to become a transparent vessel for information. This relates to the principle of neutrality, which has been central to journalism for many years. If a reader can get the necessary information from a story in the paper without thinking about the leanings or biases of the reporter, there is an assumption that the reader can trust the information as accurate.

Broadcasting is inherently different because the person presenting the news is seen and/or heard, resulting in a more complete human connection between the presenter and the audience member. The broadcasting industry converted this potential weakness into a strength by marketing its news presenters as likable, relatable personalities. As a result, it makes sense that broadcasters would personalize the news to a greater extent than newspaper reporters, often using words like "we," "us," and "you," as well as emphasizing a story's direct impact on the audience rather than taking a just-the-facts approach. With the popularity of TV, however, some newspapers have adopted similar approaches, so what used to be a big difference between print and broadcast journalism has diminished in recent years.

Stylebooks

The same

The AP Stylebook is a great resource for any journalist regardless of platform because it clarifies common questions that arise in news writing. For instance: I don't want to be repetitive, so can I alternate between referring to a serviceman as a "Marine" and as a "soldier"? The answer is "no", as they aren't interchangeable. This kind of question and thousands of others like it make the AP Stylebook indispensable. At www.apstylebook.com, you can purchase a paper copy of the book or you can sign up for an annual digital subscription for a searchable AP Style database.

Similar

AP's Stylebook rules are occasionally the same for both print and broadcast. Many hasten to point out that an AP Broadcast Stylebook is also available, but its use is not as common in broadcast newsrooms as the print version is for newspapers. This is because a broadcast script is written, first and foremost, for the person who will say the words on the air, so the primary concern is with the preferences of that person. For example, the AP Broadcast Stylebook places phonetic "pronouncers" in parentheses after the correctly spelled proper name: "Edward Kennedy (Ken-uh-dee) voted for the measure." Some broadcasters like it that way, but others find it distracting and prefer to remove the proper spelling, leaving only the phonetic pronouncer ("Edward Ken-uh-Dee voted . . . "). Print stylebooks achieve standardization, but broadcast scripts are often individualized.

Different

While the AP Stylebook is "the bible" for most print reporters, broadcast journalism lacks an equivalent book. Anchors and reporters prefer that their scripts be formatted in different ways, and whatever helps them sound as good as possible saying the words is what counts. This makes it vital that producers and anchors work together effectively. When in doubt, a producer should ask the anchor for personal

22

preferences, and it is incumbent on anchors to pre-read scripts before going on air, making corrections as needed.

Attribution

The same

Any purported statement of fact short of "the sky is blue" needs attribution. This is difficult for some new journalism students to get used to, but it is essential to the profession. Average readers might not be consciously aware of the journalism profession's rules, but they will know if you're just shooting from the hip or haven't done your homework. They'll know if you're merely stating the obvious or repeating the same ideas over and over again. They'll know if you're spouting your opinion. The way to avoid any such perception is to write tightly attributed news stories. Always ask yourself, "Says who?" If you don't know a specific answer to that question – or if the answer is "me" – you have more work to do.

Similar

The standard rule in journalism is that some form of the word "said" is preferable to its synonyms (stated, claimed, uttered) because most other words have opinionated connotations. A common expression in journalism is "'Said' (or 'says') is a good word" meaning both that it's not opinionated and that it's a benign word that doesn't get old when repeated frequently. This rule of thumb applies in both print and broadcast journalism.

"Title before name" is a rule commonly taught in broadcast news writing, but there's no rule against it in print. The idea is that "Joe Smith, district attorney" doesn't roll off the tongue as easily as "District Attorney Joe Smith." A great trick is to remove words like "of" in titles. For example, "Director of Human Relations Joe Smith" can be shortened to "Human Relations Director Joe Smith." Occasionally exceptions might arise, but generally if you see the word "of" in a title, you can probably get rid of it by slightly reordering the words.

Different

A common-sense rule in broadcasting is to put the attribution at the beginning of a sentence in order to prevent confusion regarding the source of the information. If we went on TV and said, "Jones robbed a bank, according to police," it would sound as if we stated unequivocally that he's guilty before the all-important attribution to police sources. The better approach in broadcasting would be, "Police say Jones robbed a bank." It is worth pointing out, however, that this does not amount to a difference between print and broadcasting in every case, because there's nothing wrong with attribution at the beginning of a sentence in print either. This rule is just more flexible in print.

When quoting or paraphrasing someone's words, some form of the word "said" is preferable, but the verb tense is different. Newspapers traditionally used the simple past tense "said" for the same reason they preferred the past tense in general. Radio and TV newscasts, on the other hand, are often live, so they emphasize what's going on now – even as it applies to the playing of a soundbite now. So, *said* is a good word, and so is *says*.

Punctuation

The same
The most useful punctuation marks in news writing, regardless of medium, are commas and periods. It is possible to write entire stories using only these two punctuation marks. Dashes are also useful but should not replace periods. Many people in news regard semicolons as unnecessary because they usually do the same jobs as periods.

What's good for print is often good for broadcast. A good example is hyphenating compound modifiers – cases where two words work together to modify a third, as in "well-known person" or "mid-June weekend." If you're saying the words out loud, it's important to see the hyphen so you don't accidentally pause in the wrong place ("well . . . known person").

Similar
Both print and broadcast news writers use commas, but in broadcast writing it's preferable to avoid certain kinds of expressions that require them. Appositive phrases, parenthetical expressions adding detail as in this sentence, are difficult to say out loud and sometimes trip people up on the air. As a result, many get the impression that it's wrong to use commas in broadcast writing, but this is incorrect. Commas are useful in broadcast writing for most of the same purposes as in print, but it's best to limit yourself to one major fact per sentence. "Johnson, a bricklayer from Toronto, won the lottery" would read more easily as "Johnson won the lottery. He's a bricklayer from Toronto."

Different

The most pronounced differences between print and broadcast when it comes to punctuation are best understood as common sense rather than style rules. Broadcast scripts are private documents written exclusively for the eyes of those who will say the words on the air and members of the production crew helping with the broadcast. Therefore, the script is prepared with the primary goal of helping the reporter or anchor say the words clearly and understandably without messing up.

Punctuation, therefore, gives the speaker a roadmap for how to say the words. Most commonly, this means using punctuation to denote pauses, as in this sentence. Many broadcast writers overuse commas, because they hear in their heads how they intend to deliver a given sentence. However, writers commonly use dashes or ellipses for a similar function, so the previous sentence might look like this: "Most commonly, this means using punctuation ... as a roadmap ... to denote pauses – as in this sentence."

There tend to be two camps in broadcast newsrooms – those who prefer dashes ... and those who prefer ellipses. In a print newsroom that strictly followed the AP or another stylebook, editors would institute a uniform rule for how and when to use commas, dashes, ellipses and other punctuation marks. In television, the rule is simply to ask the person who will read the copy for a personal preference.

Numbers

The same

Both print and broadcast journalists seek the best ways to maximize the information provided while keeping things short and not confusing viewers or readers. Both forms of writing prize clarity and precision above all else and this includes instances where numbers matter to a story.

Similar

Print and broadcast writers both use words for numbers one through nine and figures for higher numbers like 16 or 432. Both also use words for large numbers like "million" or "billion." Broadcasters typically follow the same rule when combining smaller and larger numbers, as in 17 million. The traditional broadcast rule takes the concept a little further, following the same principle with thousands, as in six thousand.

Different

Broadcasters try to avoid numbers whenever possible. When faced with a complex number, broadcasters will try to round the number in order to make it simpler. This is because it's unlikely that a listener will be able to process a complex number, like 18,983, while driving a car or cooking dinner. It's better simply to say "around 19 thousand." In print, on the other hand, readers have the time to stop and think about the number or reread it if they want to, so the reporter may as well be as accurate as possible.

Quotes/soundbites

The same

Quotes (in print) and soundbites (in broadcasting) add a human element to a story that goes beyond objective facts. They offer opinion, color and human experience to a story.

Print and broadcast journalists place quotes or soundbites in their stories with very little introduction. There's no need to write in a print story, "Jones had this to say . . . " because the attribution and quotation marks will make it obvious. The same is true with soundbites in broadcasting. Words like "had this to say" are a waste of space in print and a waste of time on the air.

Similar

Television news packages (edited video stories) sometimes have more soundbites than sentences delivered by the reporter, but there are no definitive rules about this. Newspaper writers and TV producers make stylistic choices determining how their stories come across, but these are developed and learned through experience. For the beginning journalist, there is no need for confusion in this regard. Quotes and soundbites serve the same journalistic function and are integrated into stories the same way.

Different

Print writers can remove vocal fillers ("um", "ya know", "like") more easily than broadcasters can. Digital editing makes it technically possible to do so, but the result is noticeable to the viewer unless more time is devoted to editing than is typically available. As a result, soundbites tend to run "as is," which can mean they contain less information than a similar length quote in a newspaper.

Story form and length

The same

Both print and broadcast newsrooms have standard lengths and story forms that are fairly consistent, but the importance of a given story also plays a role in the amount of space (print) or time (broadcast) an editor will devote to it. Generally, your editor, producer, news director or assignment-desk editor will give you an idea how long and what type of story you're being asked to deliver at the time you receive the assignment. One great thing about the Internet era in journalism, however, is that limitations on story length don't necessarily apply to Web versions. Even if you're asked for a short, 300-word, just-the-basic-facts story for your paper's print edition, you can add more information online. This is especially useful for broadcast journalists, who face greater restrictions in story length.

Different

Broadcast: A common approach to formatting a broadcast story is: Grab attention (using one short sentence or fragment); summarize key facts (either in the first or second sentence); a few more sentences answering the question, "What else do I need to know?"; and end with what happens next ("Jones will appear in court tomorrow morning") or a brief tidbit of information that's related but wasn't part of the essential "what happened" elements – like "This is the third bank robbery in Springfield since Monday."

Print: A lead summarizes the story such that a reader could conceivably read only one sentence and have the general idea of what happened. Subsequent sentences add detail. In traditional inverted pyramid form, these details are placed in descending order of importance, which really means descending order of impact on a reader's understanding of what happened.

FINAL FOUR

If you take nothing else away from this chapter, here are four things you should remember:

1 Your audience usually won't see your broadcast script, but they will see your text article. Broadcast scripts are functional for their intended purpose, which is to prepare for speaking on TV, radio or Web video, but their writers often need to tidy them up before presenting them for the readers. If you understand this, the supposed differences between print and broadcast writing become less daunting.

2 Use simple sentences: Subject (who or what), verb (did what), object (to whom, when, in what context, where, why – but not too much of this in one sentence). If you answer these clearly, you're probably doing a decent job writing news, regardless of platform.

3 Print sentences provide more detail because there's more space, whereas broadcast sentences are short and simple in order to be read smoothly in one breath and be easily understood. But writing news always means answering the following questions on behalf of your reader or viewer: What's the point? What else do I need to know to understand the story? How does it affect me? What's going to happen next? What else is interesting about the story that wasn't covered previously?

4 If you feel more comfortable writing for print or for spoken word, there's no guarantee this will change, but you don't have to fear switching back and forth. Just keep it clear, answer the key questions, always be mindful of your reader's or viewer's understanding of the information, and you'll successfully navigate the world of cross-platform writing. And remember: "Say it. Write it. Say it again."

Finding Stories

Vincent F. Filak

3

Introduction

Journalists say that one of the hardest things about the job is finding new stories each day. In the 1940s and 1950s, competition among newspapers was fierce, making it tough to find "scoops" and unique angles on important stories. Today, the number of competing media outlets is exponentially larger than it was back then so it will be even more difficult to find stories that are unique to your publication.

Great reporting requires a strong work ethic, combined with an inquisitive nature and a heavy dose of tenacity. In some cases, great stories come from an odd stroke of luck, but in most cases, you can make your own luck through some of the tips outlined below.

This chapter will explain how to have the right mindset as you pursue potential stories. It will also reveal how you can find stories in a traditional news beat as well as how you can look beyond the standard stops on a beat to get some really great news pieces.

The Audience Principle

If you want to write things people want to read, you need to find stories that people want to hear. The best way to do this is to start with the idea that you are writing for your audience, so you should shape your approach to content accordingly. You need to learn who is in your audience, what things impact those readers and what kinds of things they want to know (or need to know).

Some things are universal: Money, work, health and leisure. People of all backgrounds will likely have an interest in these topics. If you know the specific demographic and psychographic elements that apply to your readers, you can fine-tune stories on these issues. For example, how to avoid injury at work can be a simple topic, but the story will be different if you are writing for people who work desk jobs or if you are writing for construction workers.

Other things have a limited but engaged audience. How to afford college is likely an important topic for many people reading this book. However, once those people finish college, that topic won't matter as much anymore. Wedding magazines are filled with stories on how to pick a perfect dress for a certain body type and how to plan a princess-style wedding on a pauper's budget. Parenting magazines constantly reassure new parents that there is nothing wrong with children who are fussy eaters and that eventually the children will learn to use a toilet. Once the weddings are planned and the children are toilet-trained, these magazines become less useful and thus fall out of favor with that set of readers.

You need to look at the readership you are trying to serve, figure out what matters to those readers and then seek stories that will be interesting and helpful to them.

5WS AND 1H

The "5Ws and 1H" serve as the bedrock of journalistic writing, and they can also help you as you try to figure out what kinds of stories you should seek.

- Who will want to read this?
- What do I need to tell the reader?
- When does this matter to them?
- Where, in a geographic sense, will this story have the most impact?
- Why should someone read this?
- How can I appeal to this audience?

HOW TO KNOW AN AUDIENCE

Advertising and marketing professionals take audience characteristics seriously because their livelihood depends on getting the right people to see their work and buy their products. News writers, on the other hand, often decide that if they write on a topic that interests them, the resulting story will interest the readers. This mistake can alienate readers who view the journalists as self-centered and disconnected.

To reach your readers, you need to fully understand who your readers are. Here are three key things to consider when assessing an audience:

• Demographic Segmentation: Standard survey "check-box items" allow researchers to use measurable personal characteristics to divide a population into a series of specific groups. Age, race, gender, education and economic status are just some of the ways in which you can parse a population. If you understand who reads your work, you can better tailor your work to meet their needs.

For example, people in the "traditional college student" age bracket (18–24) are more likely to be interested in certain forms of technology than people in an "older adult" (65+) age bracket might be. In addition, the approach to the writing can differ, as younger individuals more readily accept less-formal writing.

If you can understand who is reading your work based on a few simple descriptors, you can fine-tune your approach to what stories you are writing and how you are writing them.

• Geographic Segmentation: The Web is a worldwide medium, but sites are often more or less popular in certain geographic regions. The content will reflect certain aspects of that area or that area's key interests.

In Madison, Wisconsin, people need to know how to dig out of their houses after a blizzard. In Madison, Georgia, residents are more likely to experience sunstroke than a blizzard. The upper peninsula of Michigan has issues with bears that dig through people's trash, while the swampier parts of Florida have issues with alligators that eat unattended pets.

Even when your readers come from various locations, your own geographic placement can lead to interesting stories. What makes your area special? What are some of the things that happen here that don't happen elsewhere? What are some of the traditions, oddities and otherwise unique elements that make your place on Earth different? In capturing those things, you can offer your readers a wider array of information and you can find a lot of stories that will entice and engage your readers.

• Psychographic Segmentation: Just because people are from the same general area or the same age group, it doesn't necessarily follow that they will have the same interests. If you have two 35-year-old men who make $50,000 a year, live in Chicago and spend 10 percent of their money on sporting events, it doesn't necessarily follow that an article on hockey will interest both of them.

Psychographics allow you to use values, attitudes and lifestyles to better understand a target audience. If you use these topics to shape your focus on an audience, you can better understand specific things that matter to your readers.

For example, college students in the United States traditionally fit into the 18- to 24-year-old age bracket, with a 44 percent to 56 percent male/female split on gender. According to the National Center for Educational Statistics (http://nces.ed.gov), the racial breakdown shows that 61 percent of the students nationwide are white, 14 percent are black, 13 percent are Hispanic and 6 percent are Asian/Pacific Islander, with the remaining 6 percent unknown or listed as "non-residents." However, not every college student is going to be interested in the same things, even if you picked a group of them from the largest chunk of each demographic category.

On the campus of Gustavus Adolphus College, a private college associated with the Evangelical Lutheran Church, one prominent campus tradition is "Case Day." This underground student event, which challenges students to consume 24 beers in a day, has been a prominent story in the college's student newspaper for a number of years, despite administrators' pleas to halt the festivities. Conversely, on the campus of Brigham Young University, a private college associated with The Church of Jesus Christ of Latter-day Saints, alcohol is not allowed, in accordance with the Mormon Church's law of health and proper diet.

Not every experience within a demographic will be the same and thus using psychographic analysis to determine the interest of people for whom you are writing will be important.

Beat Reporting

Legacy publications, such as newspapers and magazines, often divide their coverage into geographic or topical areas known as beats. Each beat is then assigned a reporter who will cover the news that occurs in that area. Media outlets use beats to help reporters familiarize themselves with the important facets of an area or topic. This approach also prevents multiple reporters from reporting on the same topics.

Many websites have a niche approach to coverage as well: ESPN.com, for example, focuses entirely on sports; ADA.org focuses on news related to oral health; and FarmersOnly.com is a dating site that serves as *The* place for farmers and ranchers to meet like-minded people." In each case, the focal point of the publication can help writers look for stories on topics that would interest the site's readers.

If you are covering a beat or working in a particular niche of journalism, you have some ready-made stories that are easy to find. Here are some ways you can use a beat-reporting approach to find stories and inform your readers.

Follow the beat

Most beats will have a clear "home base" that is obvious to a good reporter. Government reporters will start at city hall or the statehouse. Education reporters will have a school district office and schools. Crime reporters will have police precincts and a sheriff's department.

Many beats will have scheduled gatherings you should attend, such as city council meetings, school board meetings and police commission meetings. At these events, you can look for interesting stories that matter to your readers. In addition, you can introduce yourself to the important people on your beat. It is a good idea to be familiar with the administrators who work in the area that you cover. When you get to know these people, they will likely tip you off to stories.

Talk to other people

Officials are important and you should view them as crucial sources for your beat. However, you also need to look beyond the people with the fancy titles and big offices. In many cases, the people who can put you on to great stories are not the people in charge.

Secretaries, or administrative assistants, are aware of everything that comes through an office on a daily basis. If someone is being hired or fired, these folks see all the paperwork involved in the process. If someone has a plan to build or destroy something, chances are good that the secretaries have seen the blueprints or construction contracts. Secretaries also serve as gatekeepers for an office and determine who gets to see the boss and whose phone calls or emails get returned. Secretaries are vital to the day-to-day operation of most places on any beat.

The same thing is true of security guards, janitors and other people who help keep things functioning. They often see things others do not and can offer you different perspectives on things that happen on your beat. Do not treat these people poorly because you think they lack value.

In addition, talk to the people impacted by what is happening on your beat. Teachers and principals will have views on education, as

33

will parents and students. Defense attorneys and social workers can help you find stories on a court beat as often as judges and prosecutors. The more people you talk to, the wider the scope of the stories you will find.

Beats, which are also referred to as "rounds" or "patches" in some places, will vary from city to city and country to country. Here is a non-exhaustive list of areas you might find yourself covering. In some of these areas, you might have sub-specialties, such as covering a particular branch of government or a specific sport.

Government
Police and fire
Courts
Science and health
Environment
Arts and culture
Entertainment
Lower education (K–12)
Higher education (college)
Business
Faith/religion
Technology
Sports

Look at the competition and outdo them

No self-respecting journalist enjoys getting scooped on a story, but it is part of life in this field. When a competitor publishes a story that you don't have, consider it a challenge and an opportunity. Every story, no matter how well done, will have flaws. Your job is to find these flaws and fix them.

Stories often leave unexplored angles that beg for follow-up pieces. For example, if the president of your university unexpectedly retires, the first story will likely be the "who and what" piece that explains who this person was and what he or she did at the institution. The first-day story will include background on the departing president and a number of "we're sorry to see the president leave" quotes from various people.

What is missing are the "why" and "how" elements of the story: "Why" did this person decide to leave and "how" will the school fill the president's role with someone else? You can easily look for ways to fill those gaps when you follow up. You can also dig around for information on potential candidates for this job. If you keep looking ahead, you will make sure you that you are at the forefront of this story for the duration of its lifecycle.

Localize the news

Things that happen all over the world have the potential to create a direct local impact. Your job is to find a way to explain that impact and make it matter to your readers. These types of stories, known as localizations, are among the best types of stories because they are easy to conceptualize and they have direct audience appeal.

When you see stories on things like statewide initiatives or countrywide budgets, look for ways to point out what this means to people in your area. Localizations need to have value beyond mere reaction from audience members, especially if the people are not aware of what is actually happening on the broader stage. In addition, not every national or international story will have a strong local appeal. However, when you can see a clear line from the big story to your readers, whip up a local version.

35

People on people

Profile stories can give you an exciting glimpse into the lives of interesting people. Readers enjoy the life stories of other people who are like them or who have experienced things they never will. Profile subjects are like the stars of their own movies. A skilled storyteller can show that movie to a broader audience.

When selecting a profile subject, look for people who spend a lot of time in the public eye. These people can be important business CEOs or the person who has spent 45 years teaching grade school. The idea is to reveal aspects of this person's life and personality to the audience in the hope of entertaining and engaging your readers. Look for people who interest you and see if they would be willing to tell you who they are and what they do.

VIEW FROM A PRO

JAMIE BECKMAN

Jamie Beckman's road to freelance success began in Emmaus, Pennsylvania, a city with a population of just over 11,000, when she interned for Men's Health magazine. Since then, she has worked for Budget Travel, Popular Mechanics, Marie Claire, Town & Country, Redbook and USA Today's newsstand magazines, just to name a few. She is also the author of the book, "The Frisky 30-Day Breakup Guide", which was published in 2010.

Figure 3.1
Jamie Beckman.

Beckman said the key to writing for such a broad array of publications is to think about what the people in the audience will want to know.

"Before I begin a story, I always think of the reader," she said. "Who is he or she? What do these people want to get out of this piece? I write a lot of service journalism-oriented listicles: tips, tricks and hints about health, relationships, travel, beauty . . . you name it. I always try to keep in mind who I'm writing for."

To help her find ideas for freelance pitches, Beckman said she uses every aspect of her life to come up with stories.

"Once I was walking to the grocery store, and I happened to have skipped my workout that morning, and I thought to myself, 'Jeez, I wonder what it would take to get a workout out of, say, walking down the street, or carrying groceries?'" she said.

"I ended up pitching and selling the idea to Redbook. For the piece, I interviewed experts about exactly how fast you'd have to walk to work up a sweat and how you can strength-train by carrying your groceries to the car."

"You don't have to be a genius to come up with good ideas," she added. "You just have to act on the idea as soon as you have it and pitch it to an outlet that would actually be interested in it."

Over her career, Beckman has worked in traditional and digital media. She said the Web made her more nimble and writing for magazines helped her appreciate the value of the editing and revision process. However, she said, the tenets of journalism she learned in school more than a decade ago remain important.

"No matter the platform, good reporting and writing will always stand out," Beckman said. "If you're unsure about how to transition from one platform to the other, talk to your editor about expectations, story length and anything extra he or she might need."

The most important thing about finding ideas, is having faith in yourself, Beckman said. The key is to be persistent in looking for them.

"You *will* get ideas. You *will*," she said. "Try to socialize with different types of people and listen to what issues they're going through, where they're hanging out, what they can't get enough of at the moment. Also, read as much as you can and use social media to follow the news, follow crazy entertainers, follow thought leaders in your industry. . . . You don't have to be the smartest person or the best freelancer right out of the gate. Hang in there. Persevere. Then beat everyone else who gives up."

Beyond the Beats

To prevent yourself from falling into a rut, you will need to look into some things that go beyond the standard fare of event coverage and rewriting press releases. If you get into the field as a freelancer, you will also be responsible for generating your own story ideas so you can pitch them to editors at a variety of publications. Below are some suggestions that can be helpful to you if you are on a beat or on your own.

37

Read everything

If you follow the advice of Jamie Beckman (see the "View from a Pro" box in this chapter), you should look at everything around you as a potential story idea. One of the best ways to find the ideas is to read anything you can get your hands on.

General trends, big news items and other things you find in the daily papers and on well-trodden websites can give you some basic ideas, but if you look at other, less-common bits of text, you can find great stories. Reading the back of a cereal box can make you wonder, "Who writes the copy for the kiddie games on these things?" Reading through your junk mail can clue you into the latest scams going through people's inboxes. Reading graffiti can lead you to a historical piece on how tagging began and why it initially had a useful purpose. This kind of curiosity can have you interviewing cereal manufacturers, Internet detectives and vandalism experts. It can also lead to some engaging stories.

If you want to pitch a piece to a particular publication, Beckman suggests you read at least the past three issues of the publication so you can understand its audience and the tone it takes with the readers. You can also use this as an opportunity to discover what that publication has already done and then expand it, localize it or contradict it. The more you read, the more chances you have to find a topic of interest.

Sourcing yourself

As much as you aren't writing for yourself, you do have a number of traits, skills and experiences that are universal. When you need to find story ideas, look inside yourself for things that you are doing, or have done, that might be worth sharing with other people. When you find these topics, look for ways to make them more universal so that your readership can relate to your work.

If you got a parking ticket at a broken meter, you might feel compelled to write about this as an issue of fairness. However, your ticket probably isn't the only one of this kind. Interviews with other people who park in the area, police officers who ticket cars and legal experts who deal in these issues can help you widen the scope of the story beyond your experience. This will help readers relate to the topic and draw a larger audience to your story.

I AM

When you need an idea, look to some of your own experiences and ask some basic questions. These can send you down a road that gives you promising leads.

- What are my hobbies?
- What stresses me out?
- Where have I worked?
- What do I do that I think is easy but others are amazed by?
- How am I different now as opposed to X years ago?
- What was the most important toy I got as a child?
- What do I do every day?
- Where have I lived?

Stop tuning out

The prevalence of portable electronic devices gives people an opportunity to carry a library of entertainment with them wherever they go. Smart phones, digital music players and e-readers allow people to disappear into their own world while waiting for a bus or walking across campus. As fun as they can be, these devices prevent you from seeing story ideas.

The next time you go somewhere, unplug yourself from these digital distractions and really look at the things happening around you. Bulletin boards and kiosks around campus are filled with potential story ideas just waiting to be discovered. As you take a walk around the city, you might notice new businesses cropping up or construction happening in your area. You might overhear a conversation between two people who are walking in front of you or see a growing trend in how people are dressing. The more attuned you stay to the world, the more likely you are to find odd stories in unlikely moments.

View things with wonder

Comedian Dana Carvey said his son once asked him, "Daddy, does God have feet?" The question lacks pretense. It lacks fear of mockery. Best of all, it isn't even close to the weirdest question rattling around in the head of a child. Somewhere along the way, we stop wondering where the stars go in the daytime or if fish can drown. The daily grind of life and the fear of sounding stupid limit our ability to engage in wonder.

If you want to find great stories, ask the favorite question of all children: "Why?" Some of the best stories come from wondering why things are the way they are. Malcolm Gladwell wrote a piece for The New Yorker called "The Ketchup Conundrum" that touched on the evolution of condiments, the sensory perception of taste and food marketing over time. The question that launched his tale was simple: We have dozens of types of mustard. Why do we really only have one type of ketchup?

Simple "why" questions can lead to incredibly fun and rewarding stories. Besides, if you are wondering about the topic, it is a safe bet you aren't alone in your puzzlement.

Be nosy

A good journalism instructor can teach you everything aside from how to be nosy. Nosy people tend to make the best journalists because they dig into almost every topic and ask almost any question. When you are at a coffee shop, eavesdrop on someone else's conversation. When you are in the line at a store and you hear two strangers talking about something that interests or irritates them, join in. In some cases, the things you learn will reinforce ideas you already have ("Why isn't

39

there more parking on this campus?") while in other cases, you might be introduced to a whole new world ("Did you know there's a class you can take that teaches you how to be a circus clown?"). The more you can intersect with the lives of other people, the more likely it is you will find some quality story ideas.

FIVE WEIRD QUESTIONS THAT COULD BE STORIES

Is there a group of FBI agents that does nothing but check if people have copied old VHS tapes or DVDs? At the front of every movie, there is a threat from the FBI and Interpol and anyone else noting how copying and distributing tapes is a crime. Has anyone ever been busted for moving tapes to DVDs for their own use? If this branch of government does exist, what is life like as one of these intrepid G-Men who is on "movie patrol"?

Why can't the United States develop a popular dollar coin? Across the European Union, the Euro comes in coin form. In Canada, the "loonie" is so widely recognized, the country's mint secured rights to the term. The pound in Britain is also circulated heavily in coin form. Since the 1970s, the U.S. has gone through the Eisenhower dollar, the Susan B. Anthony dollar, the Sacagawea dollar and a series of presidential dollar coins. Despite the various attempts to make these coins work as common currency, paper dollars remain the more popular choice. Why?

How do police learn to deal with inebriated people? Drunk people are like snowflakes: No two are exactly alike. Some are violent and some are docile. Some are loud and others fall asleep in between sentences. Law enforcement officials are required to deal with intoxicated people at a fairly steady rate. How do they prepare for this? In some districts, police departments recruit citizens for a "drunk academy," where they volunteer to drink to certain points of intoxication to help train newer police. In other cases, the police are required to rely on books and ride-along training. How does your area do this?

How does someone campaign for coroner? In many small towns and various counties, the job of coroner is still an elected position. Campaign signs pop up for various candidates, although it is often an uncontested election. Still, the question remains, how does the candidate convince others to vote for him or her?

What is the weirdest thing you can buy for $20 at a yard sale or flea market? People have various forms of taste when it comes to how they dress, how they decorate and what they value. A yard sale is a chance to get an inside look at the personal items of a wide array of people. Any weekend with decent weather can lead to rummage sales, yard sales, garage sales and other similar venues. Get out there and see what's available.

FINAL FOUR

If you take nothing else away from this chapter, here are four things you should remember:

1 **You should keep your focus on your audience**. You can use what you see, hear and experience to find story ideas, but your search should not start and stop with you. Keep your audience in mind when you look for stories and when you write them. The more you keep the focus on your readers, the better your work will be.

2 **Everything can become a story**. Ideas both large and small have led to stories that draw readers and make for interesting conversation pieces. Keep working on an idea even if you don't think it is worth anything on first glance. Give it a chance to develop.

41

3 **Pay attention**. The less time you spend in your own little world, the more things you will see happening around you. If you open the aperture on your mental lens, you can let in a lot of great ideas that will lead to many incredible stories.

4 **Persistence is key**. The adage of "If at first you don't succeed, try, try again" applies here as you look for stories. Just because the first editor didn't like the story idea or your first source wasn't all that great, it doesn't mean the next editor won't like it or the next source won't be great. Don't give up easily.

Reporting Beyond the Basics

Scott Reinardy

Introduction

Oramel Barrett was a newspaperman. Born in Norwich, Vermont, he enjoyed political journalism, criticized American wars and disliked the government's assault on civil liberties.

Everything in the above paragraph is true. However, it does not represent the entire truth. Barrett owned a Democratic-leaning newspaper in Harrisburg in the mid-19th century that opposed the Civil War, oftentimes distorting facts to support his cause.

Barrett's most notable journalistic faux pas came in November 1863. As the owner and editor of the Harrisburg Patriot & Union, he wrote:

> We pass over the silly remarks of the president. For the credit of the nation we are willing that the veil of oblivion shall be dropped over them and that they shall be no more repeated or thought of.
>
> (Patriot & Union, 1863)

Understanding the miscalculation of Barrett's editorial on President Abraham Lincoln's "Gettysburg Address," the Patriot & Union's successor newspaper, the Harrisburg Patriot-News, published a retraction on Nov. 14, 2013, writing:

Seven score and ten years ago, the forefathers of this media institution brought forth to its audience a judgment so flawed, so tainted by hubris, so lacking in the perspective history would bring, that it cannot remain unaddressed in our archives.

(Patriot-News Editorial Board, 2013)

Barrett's story is riddled with a multitude of journalistic lessons but none as resounding as a lesson in good reporting. If he had done his reporting, no one would need to apologize for Barrett's work 150 years after the fact.

This chapter will build upon basic reporting tactics. It will examine issues such as fact gathering, the value of information, online research and access to material. It also will provide you with some tools to find, evaluate and use the things you gather when developing your story.

Reporting vs. Writing

In the hyperactive information age, we are bombarded with messages much of our waking lives. Some research suggests that on average we consume more than 15 hours of media per day (Zverina, 2013). Our job as journalists is to distinguish good information from bad, and determine what is truthful, accurate and fair.

A few years ago, a couple of former sports writers complained that ESPN's SportsCenter had altered sports language for the worse.

Reporters must distinguish between facts and suppositions, opinions and ideals. Here are some tips for identifying facts:

- A fact is something that is verifiable through many sources.
- A fact is a piece of information that is generally agreed upon.
- A fact comes from a reliable source.
- A fact is based in evidence found through research.
- A fact is accurate.
- A fact refutes falsehoods.
- A fact welcomes scrutiny.
- A fact is not an unverifiable opinion.
- A fact does not generate from an unreliable source.
- A fact does not lack truth.
- A fact accepts open debate and discussion, but still remains a fact.

Words such as "Yahtzee" were used by sports anchors to describe home runs and "taking it to the house" was now a touchdown. The former sports writers conducted research asking sports editors how reporting had changed in light of the entertaining use of language.

Overwhelmingly the sports editors complained that sports writers were trying to "write their way through stories" instead of relying on good reporting. One sports editor said, "I think writers sometimes go for flair over solid reporting. In other words, too much 'boo-yeah' and not enough meat and potatoes." Another said, "Reporters try too hard to be clever, rather than letting the facts tell the story" (Reinardy and Perry, 2005).

National syndicated columnist Leonard Pitts has long argued that in the United States, people's beliefs have overcome the acceptance of facts:

> If you and I had an argument, and I produced facts from an authoritative source to back me up, you couldn't just blow that off. You might try to undermine my facts, might counter with facts of your own, but you couldn't just pretend my facts had no weight or meaning.
>
> (Pitts, 2010)

45

Reporting is the act of fact gathering. As responsible, reliable and trustworthy journalists, we must make facts the core of our work. Before journalists write, they need to report.

Information Hunters and Gatherers

Information comes from many sources. Press releases provide information, as do newspapers, websites and cereal boxes. Here are a few common sources of information that good journalists use to find facts and gather information:

The Internet

This instrument is mostly used as a secondary source. Google, Yahoo, Bing and others are search engines, not sources. Search engines can lead a reporter to a lot of information. Assessing the quality of the information is another issue we'll discuss later. As a secondary source, online information.

- Gives reporters a starting point for finding facts.
- Provides information that can be verified with a primary source. Primary sources generally include people.

- Sometimes provides information that can be used in a story as a primary source, such as a company's mission statement. However, the information has to be properly cited.

Organizations

Businesses, political groups, sports teams and other organizations all want to send their messages to the public. Most of the messages are positive statements that support the mission of the group. As a journalist, your job is to provide an unvarnished version of the truth, which can put you at odds with these institutions. When you seek information from these organizations, you should verify it with material from other sources and "live" sources within the organizations.

Social media

Websites such as Facebook, Twitter, LinkedIn, and Pinterest can be great secondary sources of information. Again, you should speak to a "live" source to confirm information you find on the site. Here are some questions to ask about secondary-source information:

- Who is the original source of the information?
- Has someone taken responsibility for the information?
- Can the information be verified with other sources?
- Is the information a fact or an opinion?
- Will others refute the information with facts of their own?
- What are the biases of the source?
- What is the motivation of a source to provide information?

Simply because something was "liked" or "retweeted" a billion times does not make it a journalistically solid piece of information.

"Real People" vs. "Public Officials"

Human beings are the most common primary sources for stories. Public Officials are elected and appointed local, state and federal government officials. They can be great sources of information, but again, a word of caution: Most politicians want to be re-elected and city officials want to keep their jobs. So while their words are useful, Public Officials oftentimes speak from a biased perspective. Real People are those who are generally caught in the works of Public Officials. Real People help put a face to the story. Some action, be it a tornado, chemical spill or a smoking ban, affects Real People. Every story should include Real People. If state politicians decide to enact a bill that would ban teenagers from using commercial tanning beds, how would that affect high school students preparing for prom? How would it affect the local tanning salon business owner? What would the ban do to local taxes collected from tanning salons?

Whether you include Public Officials or Real People in stories, all sources need to be carefully vetted. All information collected needs to be viewed through a skeptical eye. Ask these questions:

- What is this person's stake in the story? What does he or she have to lose or gain?
- Who else can confirm or refute the information this source provides?
- Who has an opposing viewpoint?
- Is the source's information reasonable? For instance, if a source says a new light bulb will burn for 20 years, ask if there is any science or research that can support that claim.
- Did the source contact you or did you contact the source? Sometimes sources have biased perspectives and will reach out to the media to tell their stories. Proceed with caution and ask, "Does the source have an ax to grind or a vendetta?" If a worker at a local pizza parlor says the owner hasn't paid her in weeks, what evidence can she provide? A reporter would certainly want to ask, "Why did you continue to work if you weren't getting paid?" She might have been fired and she is trying to discredit the shop's owner. Or she might not have been paid and the owner has a history of cheating workers. Check with the state's Better Business Bureau to see if formal complaints have been filed against the business owner.

47

Sources of information are nearly endless: Overheard grocery story conversations, posters, billboards, advertisements, public message boards online and on location, junk mail, email spam, flyers tacked to telephone poles, classified ads, your mom, your friends and you. These are generally secondary sources, but secondary sources lead to primary sources. And for each source a reporter interviews, he or she should ask for additional sources.

One quick note about personal observations: Although you might be a trusted source, you should verify the information and the things

VIEW FROM A PRO

ERIC ADLER

When Kansas City Star senior reporter Eric Adler interviews a source for a story, he makes two promises.

"I usually promise I will do my best to understand your life and be as accurate in my writing in both fact and spirit," he said. "Not just what you say, the facts of your life, but the spirit in which you say it and what it means."

As an award-winning journalist, Adler develops rapport with sources in an effort to delve deep into their stories. His two-part promise is only one part of building rapport.

"Every individual has a deep desire to be heard and recognized," he said. "People often ask, 'Why do people tell you what they tell? Or why do they talk with you at all?' What underlines that answer is people want to know they matter and that what they're going through is important."

Figure 4.1
Eric Adler.

When teaching journalism classes at the University of Kansas, in large letters Adler will write "Genuine Interest" on the dry-erase board. He repeatedly instructs the students to be genuinely interested in the people they interview. It cannot be faked. It cannot be done half-heartedly.

"This is their story, not my story," he said. "This is not me or about my writing or what I think of you or what I feel about you. It has to do with you."

For instance, a reporter arrives at a traffic accident. Standing near the mangled debris of cars is an accident victim. Adler says the reporter should first ask, "Are you OK?" It's personal, it's caring and shows genuine interest in the victim's wellbeing. The reporter can follow with, "Wow! The car's a mess. What happened?" After listening carefully and intently, the reporter can extract other facts such as name, age, hometown, where he or she was going, etc.

"First there's that connection of, 'How are you? I'm interested. Are you all right?'"

Adler's other suggestions for building rapport are:

- Be transparent: Adler will show sources his notebook to assure them he's getting the story right.
- Find commonality: Adler will attempt to find common ground between him and his sources. He used the example of talking with a parent who has lost a child: "I've never, ever lost a child but you can sense the pain that person's going through or holding back on that pain or trying to express that pain. You say, 'I've had losses in my life. To be honest

with you those things devastated me and they are nothing, nothing compared to what I imagine you're going through. I can't relate to you and I don't think anyone can.' Then you ask, 'Do people sometimes try to relate to you?' Their response is, 'Oh yeah, people say all sorts of stupid things.' Then they open up in a sense that, 'Yeah, people don't understand.' It's not as if I can understand but I understand that I can't understand."

- Listen carefully, intently, respectfully. "A lot of times I will stop an interview long before another person will stop it. I'll say, 'You've shared a lot, maybe more than you expected to share. Can I call you later and talk more?' They need time to process it." By stopping the interview Adler builds trust with the source and demonstrates a concern for that person.
- Don't judge others. "Life is a path. Everyone gets to where they are through different paths. I want them to share their path so I never judge."

you observe. For instance, if you arrive at a car accident, and three people are pulled from a car and sustained injuries, the police report can verify that information. But what if you say two cars were totaled? The police report would not provide that information. An insurance adjustor would eventually determine the damage to the cars but for your deadline story, that information would not yet be verifiable. It's a small detail but getting small details wrong can lead to big corrections.

49

The Value of Information

Information is a commodity, a product not much different than hamburgers, gasoline or music downloads. For journalists, people with information are valued sources. The reporter has two responsibilities when considering sources:

1 Determine which sources can provide the most valuable information.
2 Determine what information is of greatest use in telling the story.

If we were to develop a hierarchy of sources – least important to most important – it would resemble an archer's target. The larger, exterior rings of the target would represent background and secondary, non-quotable sources with the smaller, interior rings representing more valuable quotable and primary sources.

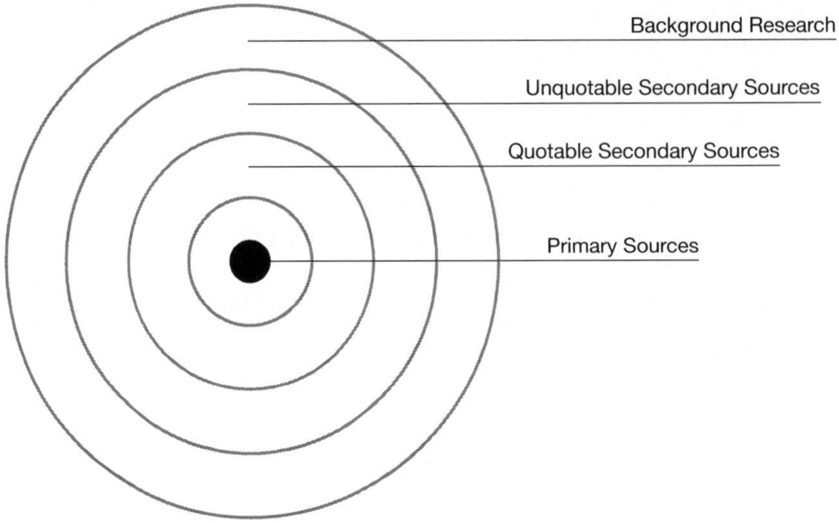

Background Research

Unquotable Secondary Sources

Quotable Secondary Sources

Primary Sources

Figure 4.2 *This target represents the series of sources you will use as you do your reporting. At the center are primary sources, which are the most important components of all good journalism.*

Prioritizing sources is essential to good reporting. The complication lies in determining which sources score on the outer edges of the target and which hit the bull's eye. A few steps in measuring the value of sources include:

- Making a list of possible sources. Sources will include a variety of types: Public Officials, Real People, victims, witnesses, perpetrators, officials, instigators, bystanders and so forth. Creating a list of all the possible sources will help identify the story's stakeholders.
- Determining who are the primary stakeholders. Stakeholders are individuals who have the most to lose or the most to gain by an action. Other stakeholders include those who will be affected by the action. These stakeholders are usually Real People that help "put a face to the story." That means, it allows the audience to see the actual outcomes of an action. Also, these Real People stakeholders are great sources for story leads. The audience feels a connection to them and their circumstances.

Measuring the value of sources means determining the secondary sources. In the target diagram, there are two kinds of secondary sources: Unquotable Secondary Sources and Quotable Secondary Sources.

> ## QUESTIONING STAKEHOLDERS
>
> Stakeholders are people who will be affected by a course of action. When attempting to determine who will be most affected by an action (primary stakeholders) you should start by asking a few questions:
>
> - Who brought this action to light? That can include, but is not limited to, a politician who introduces a bill, a firefighter working a house fire or car accident, a police detective investigating a crime, a school board member who proposes a student dress code, a religious leader who leads a protest against gay marriage, a local business owner who starts a program to educate the homeless, a homemaker who organizes a local food drive, etc. These are the people who will be at the center of the action.
> - What are the motivations of the primary stakeholders? For firefighters, police and others working in civil service, the motivation is rather obvious: A fire needs to be extinguished, a life needs to be saved, a crime needs to be solved, order needs to overcome chaos.
> - But for other stakeholders, questions need to be asked, such as:
>   - Why does the school board member want a student dress code?
>   - Why does the religious leader oppose gay marriage?
>   - Why does the business owner think the homeless need to be educated?
>   - Why does the homemaker feel compelled to start a food drive?

51

Unquotable Secondary Sources (USS) are just that – they are not to be used as named sources in the story. These are sources who want to provide information but remain anonymous. In exchange for information, they ask not to be quoted or named in the story. Even though they are not to be included in the story, the information from these sources is invaluable. Some USS include:

- Behind-the-scenes employees such as secretaries, custodians, maintenance personnel, security guards and other people who work in relative obscurity. They usually don't want to be quoted in stories for fear of losing their jobs. However, they also realize that the information they have is of value. The problem is that it's left to the reporter to track down a primary source to confirm this information. Sometimes individuals who are usually USS are in fact willing to be quoted. For example, using a security guard as a primary source when the business where he works was robbed is not only acceptable but expected.

- Other Unquotable Secondary Sources include people on the fringes of an organization or an event who, again, don't want to be quoted. These can be spectators at a tragic event such as a car accident or fire, office personnel who work closely with government officials and rank-and-file workers who are affected by a policy. Generally, the sources are between the Public Officials and the behind-the-scenes workers. These sources know enough information to be quoted but because of fear of reprisals (being punished by bosses, ostracized by fellow employees, rejected by friends or shunned by family) refuse to go "on the record."

To retain trust and credibility, a reporter will always honor an agreement he or she has made with an Unquotable Secondary Source. Failure to do so will destroy the reporter's reputation and reduce the opportunity to find cooperative sources in the future. The best course of action is to take information gathered from a USS and confirm it with a Primary Source. For example, a reporter can approach a Primary Source and say, "Sources are telling me that the mayor is resigning. Is that true?" The Primary Source might ask, "Who are these sources?" The reporter would say, "I cannot reveal my sources. Is the mayor resigning?"

Again, information is a commodity. If a reporter has good information, and can leverage that to gain other information, the story will be more complete. Quotable Secondary Sources (QSS) are sources willing to be quoted on the record but are not at the heart of the story.

For instance, teachers or parents could be QSS in the student dress-code story, members of the congregation in the anti-gay marriage rally story, other business owners in the homeless education story and other homemakers or food-drive leaders in the food-drive story. While those sources have important perspectives, those perspectives are less important and valuable than the Primary Sources.

Quotable Secondary Sources might appear to be more valuable than Unquotable Secondary Sources but that's not always the case. Sources

PROBLEMS WITH SOURCES

As a reporter, your goal is to get as close to the truth as possible. When you rely on sources, you are allowing other people to help you find the truth. However, not every source will be helpful in this regard, so you have to be careful with the information you get from sources. Source information can be problematic for many reasons:

- Sources provide conflicting information. One Primary Source says climate change is causing extreme weather and another Primary Source says it isn't. While a reporter will report both perspectives, he or she should check the science and research. What does it say? Also, the reporter should check with the general opinion of groups of researchers and include them in the story.

- Sources have agendas. They want their message heard and sometimes will say anything to get the message out. Don't fall into this trap. Extreme language, particularly in politics, is used to generate fear or at the very least get people riled up. Be wary of extremism. Good journalism does not come from people from opposite sides of an issue screaming at each other. Your job is to work through the noise and get to the issue.

- Sources will lie. There is no honor code or written agreement when a reporter interviews a source. Other than some sense of moral code, a source is not obligated to tell the truth. While many sources will be truthful, some will lie. Check and double-check information provided by a source. Secondary sources can help in fact checking. You also need to ask follow-up questions such as, "Explain how that will work?" or "How do you know that?" or "Another source told me something different. How do you respond to that?"

- Sources make mistakes. Sometimes, sources say things they don't mean or say things because they want to seem smart. They will answer questions they are unqualified to answer. No one wants to appear to be out of the loop. When asked a question, humans will answer, even if their answers are ridiculous. For example, when Gallup Polling asked more than 1,700 people about the national healthcare bill, it interchanged the words "Obamacare" and the "Affordable Care Act," even though the two represent the same bill. The poll showed that 45 percent of the respondents supported the "Affordable Care Act" but only 38 percent of the same group supported "Obamacare." Even though respondents did not know it was the same bill with two different names, they still answered the questions (Gallup, 2013).

One final tip: Be skeptical of all information. As national columnist Leonard Pitts suggests, stack facts atop each other to find the truth. If source information cannot be stacked, truth will remain elusive. The job of the reporter is to interview the sources who have those facts.

willing to be quoted or cited in a story might also be more cautious with information. An Unquotable Secondary Source does not have any restrictions on what is said, as long as the source can trust the reporter not to breach their agreement.

At the bull's eye, we'll find Primary Sources (PS). Primary Sources are the primary stakeholders. They are at the epicenter of the story. They are the most valued of sources and have the most valuable information. If information were a precious metal, Primary Sources would be gold. A story that does not include PS, or the correct primary stakeholders, is not a story.

These sources can confirm information gathered during research or interviewing Unquotable and Quotable Secondary Sources. In fact, information from secondary sources should always be confirmed with primary sources.

Online Reporting

As mentioned earlier, search engines are not sources but tools. To find or confirm information, journalists need to first develop a search strategy. A reporter's search strategy includes some of the things listed below.

Good journalists will identify the correct search instrument to find the information they want. Common domain name suffixes include .com for commercial organizations, .gov for government, .edu for education, .net for network. But since fall 2013, the Internet Corporation for Assigned Names and Numbers (ICANN) is rolling out 1,400 more suffixes. The generic Top-Level Domains, as ICANN calls them, includes just about everything imaginable such as .construction, .florist and .email. Reporters writing stories about spring break trips or winter cruises might want to check out websites with .flights, .cruises or .vacation suffixes.

Reporters should also understand which questions to ask. Is the question, "Where are college students going for spring break?" or "How much do college students spend on spring break trips?" The reporter probably wants the answer to both questions. A search that answers one question will not necessarily answer the other.

Researchers who are used to using Internet searches understand how to use key search words and phrases to narrow the search. Nouns are better for searching than other parts of speech and specifics are better

USEFUL WEBSITES

When you are looking for information online, one of the most important things is to make sure that you are relying on trustworthy websites. Here is a list of some quality websites that can help you in your reporting:

- CDC.gov: The Centers for Disease Control and Prevention is a federal site dedicated to U.S. health and disease information.
- Census.gov: Local, state and national census data is available but the census site is about more than just populations. It includes analysis of the data that includes births, marriages, minority groups and deaths.
- Opensecrets.org: A federal website that provides fundraising information on the 435 House of Representative members and the 100 senators.
- Followthemoney.org: This site is similar to Opensecrets but it provides information about individual state politicians.
- SBA.gov: The Small Business Association is a federal site that provides information about small U.S. businesses.
- GAO.gov: The Government Accountability Offices works as an independent congressional office that issues reports on how government money is spent.
- USDA.gov: The United States Department of Agriculture monitors agriculture issues such as food inspection and recalls, and crop and livestock management.
- FDA.gov: The Food and Drug Administration regulates food but it also regulates prescription and non-prescription drugs, vaccines, medical devices, cosmetics, tobacco and veterinary products.

than generalities. For instance, "spring break destinations in Mexico" is far more specific than "spring break destinations."

Social media sites usually have internal search engines. So, if a reporter is searching for college students on spring break, typing in the college name and spring break should yield results. Students can then be contacted through their social media page. Reporters who do not want to publicly post messages to these students might be able to contact them through the college's Internet mail account.

Access to Information

The First Amendment of the United States Constitution does not guarantee journalists the right to gather information. So while your rights to speak, publish, assemble, practice religion and petition the government are protected, how you obtain information is not. Nonetheless, a number of tools provide you with access to information and assist in reporting.

For reporters, access can be defined in many ways. Physical space is one area of access. As a reporter, you need to know where you can stand while covering a house fire and how close you can get to a car accident. Other areas of access include recording telephone conversations, shooting video of outdoor seating at a street-side café and attending school board meetings. Access extends to situations where you approach people – students in the schoolyard, shoppers in a mall, homes of crime victims or police or firefighters working an accident scene.

Answers to these situations are not absolute, but here are some guidelines.

Breaking news scenes

One of the first job responsibilities young reporters receive is to cover breaking news. Editors often tell reporters to rush to fire, crime and accident scenes. But what happens when the reporter arrives? When a reporter arrives on site, he or she should immediately begin reporting.

When gathering information, consider:

- Who is in charge? Look for a police captain or fire chief at the scene who can provide information. Sometimes an information officer will be on scene to assist journalists. If you cannot identify the commander, you should approach the person giving instructions. "Approach" does not mean get in the way. Emergency responders have work to do. Let them do their work. Carrying or displaying a media identification badge is strongly suggested. This allows people at the scene to know you are a reporter.
- Where can a reporter go? Inside the "caution" tape is generally out of bounds for non-essential personnel. Unless an official allows you inside the tape, stay on the exterior, but don't be afraid to ask an officer if you can enter the area. The worst that can happen is the official says, "No." Standing on public property allows you

to report anything that is seen or heard. If it happens in a public forum that is open to anyone, you can report it. If an emergency occurs on private property, you can proceed to where the rescue crew is located. If a factory is ablaze, it becomes a public event to a certain degree. But as with all locations, if police ask you to leave or move back from a scene, the general rule is to abide by the request. Better yet, you might say, "I'll leave without argument but can I contact you later to receive some information?" Try to build rapport with emergency officials. They are invaluable sources of information.

- Who can the reporter talk with on the scene? People standing closest to the scene are probably involved in some capacity, either as victims or witnesses. Look for people the police interview because if they matter to the police, they likely have some value to you. Seek out people who appear to be involved in some way. Here's a word of caution: Don't be a vulture. Reporters are criticized for their callous treatment of people, particularly those who are already hurting. A good reporter is a person first and a reporter second. Be polite and courteous. Gently say, "I'm a reporter with the newspaper/TV station/website. I'm really sorry for (whatever it is that happened). Would you be willing to talk with me?" Be genuine. Don't fake empathy or sympathy. Don't say, "I have a job to do" or "The public has a right to know." Remember, people are not required to talk to reporters. If people refuse your request, simply say, "Thank you. Again, I'm sorry for (whatever it is that happened)." Although the source might not speak now, he or she will remember how you acted.

57

Other access issues

The rules for reporting in other physical spaces are dictated by state and local laws, although the laws can be nebulous in some cases. To help you understand how things work in a general sense, here are some answers to questionable areas:

- Can you record telephone conversations? Yes, phone conversations can be recorded in the United States but it's not that simple. States have one-party or all-party consent laws. No states allow a third party to record a conversation. In other words, if you are not involved in the conversation, you cannot record it.

- One-party consent law: At least one person having the phone conversation is aware that the conversation is being recorded. In this case, if you are recording the conversation, it's legal without notifying the source. One-party consent states include 38 states and the District of Columbia.
- All-party consent law: All parties involved in the telephone conversation have to be aware the conversation is being recorded. All-party consent states include California, Connecticut, Florida, Illinois, Maryland, Massachusetts, Michigan, Montana, Nevada, New Hampshire, Pennsylvania and Washington.

The safest way to be sure you are not breaking the law is to ask the source if it is acceptable to record the conversation. If a source is reluctant, you can say, "I don't want to make any mistakes." Most sources understand that recording a conversation is standard journalism practice. For more information about recording phone conversations, see the Reporters Committee for the Freedom of the Press at www.rcfp.org/rcfp/orders/docs/RECORDING.pdf.

- Can you shoot video of people dining at an outdoor restaurant? If you are standing on public property (street, sidewalk, public parking lot), you can videotape outdoor dining, even if it's a private restaurant. The courts have ruled that the expectation of privacy is lower when people are in common public view.
- Can you attend school board meetings? School board, city council, county commission and other government meetings are open to the public. Sometimes, those groups go into executive session to discuss issues not open to the public, such as the firing of a worker or other personnel issues. Reporters and the public are not allowed in those closed sessions.
- Are you allowed to enter schoolyards to talk with students? Reporters cannot talk to children in a schoolyard without permission. Children are minors and cannot give consent to an interview. Also, schools have security measures to ensure strangers do not enter the school or schoolyard. A reporter should abide by these measures. The general rule for young children, or even high school students, is to ask permission of school officials.
- Are you allowed to interview mall shoppers? Reporters can try to interview mall shoppers – until security decides to intervene. The best plan of action is to ask mall management if you can approach

shoppers. The same rule applies for entering any business to interview people. It's common journalistic courtesy to ask permission. Talking with people in the parking lot might be an option, but, again, asking for permission is the best approach.

- Can you knock on the door of a crime victim? This is perfectly acceptable, and actually encouraged. Victims of crimes are the best sources for information. Be polite and victims most often are willing to talk with you.
- Can you approach police or firefighters at the scene of an incident? Yes, but only those who are not fully engaged in doing their jobs. As mentioned earlier, look for those in charge who might have a minute or two to provide some information. If the official tells the reporter it is not a good time to talk, the reporter needs to respect that.

These are just some access issues you might face as a reporter. When in doubt about access, you need to talk with your editor. You need to always remember that you are trying to extract information from valuable sources, who might not want to be interviewed. Respect breeds respect. Even if a source does not talk at that time, your actions could determine if the source will submit to an interview later.

FINAL FOUR

If you take nothing else away from this chapter, here are four things you should remember:

1 Reporting is the soul of a story. Good reporting leads to good stories. Reporting is excavating for information. It requires the curiosity of an archeologist, the tenacity of a dog with a bone and the thoroughness of a medical examiner working a murder case. Do not cheat on the reporting.

2 Information is a commodity. It has value. Good reporters discover where that information is located and how to retrieve it.

3 There are good sources of information and there are bad sources of information. Learn to identify the difference. Reporters make the distinction by talking with many sources (on and off the record), double- and triple-checking information and always asking difficult questions. If something seems unusual, conduct more investigation to find out for certain.

4 Good reporting leads to truthful, accurate and fair stories. Reputations are won and lost on a reporter's reporting. And it's not just the reporter's reputation at stake. Poor reporting taints all journalists. When a reporter fails to get correct information, all journalists will pay the price.

References

Dahlen, R. L. (1998). "Harrisburg's civil war *Patriot & Union*: Its conciliatory viewpoint collapses." Retrieved from: http://housedivided.dickinson.edu/library/Dahlen1998.pdf

Facebook (2014). "About." Retrieved from: www.facebook.com/facebook/info

Gallup (2013). "What's in a name? Affordable Care Act vs. Obamacare." Retrieved from: http://pollingmatters.gallup.com/2013/11/whats-in-name-affordable-care-act-vs.html

Patriot-News Editorial Board (2013). "Retraction for our 1863 editorial calling Gettysburg Address 'silly remarks': Editorial." November 14. Retrieved from: www.pennlive.com/opinion/index.ssf/2013/11/a_patriot-news_editorial_retraction_the_gettysburg_address.html

Patriot & Union (1863). "Editorial: A voice from the dead." November 24. Reprinted on PennLive. Retrieved from: www.scribd.com/doc/184197750/Patriot-Union-Editorial-1863-On-the-Gettysburg-Address

Pitts, L. (2010). "Don't confuse them with facts." *Seattle Times*. February 21. Retrieved from: http://seattletimes.com/html/editorialsopinion/2011132171_pitts21.html

Reinardy, S., & Perry, E. L. (2005). "Boo-yah! Sports journalists identify ESPN's impact on sports writing." Association for Education in Journalism and Mass Communication, Radio-Television Journalism Division. Presented August.

Zverina, J. (2013). "U.S. Media Consumption to Rise to 15.5 Hours a Day – Per Person – by 2015." November 6. Retrieved from: http://ucsdnews.ucsd.edu/pressrelease/u.s._media_consumption_to_rise_to_15.5_hours_a_day_per_person_by_2015

Structure and Storytelling

Vincent F. Filak

Introduction

In newspapers, we call them "pieces." Online, we call them "articles." In broadcast, we call them "packages." Regardless of the field or the jargon, these things are all stories and, for them to be effective, we need to use quality storytelling as we communicate our messages.

Storytelling is a skill and art as old as humankind. Whether we are talking about ancient people who gathered around the fire to tell the stories of a triumphant hunt or discussing a novel we just finished reading, stories have a number of key elements. Stories must grab our attention. Stories can't get too long or repetitive. Stories should give us a sense of finality when they are done. Good storytellers know how to apply their skills to help tell stories.

In this chapter, we will outline the key elements to good storytelling, including things that make for great stories and things that lead to bad stories. We will also explain how successful and engaging stories should start, continue and end. Finally, we will discuss various formats of storytelling and explain which ones work best for what types of stories.

Basic Rules of Storytelling

Regardless of your field or your area of interest, a number of simple rules will help you improve your approach to storytelling. These aren't mind-blowing revelations, but before you decide to put pen to paper or your fingers to the keyboard, think about these basic maxims:

If you wouldn't read it, don't write it

One thing that happens when you flip to the "journalist" side of the storytelling relationship is you tend to forget what it's like on the "reader" side. The purpose of journalism is to engage the audience members with good writing and inform them with important information. You should keep the audience at the forefront of your mind whenever you write an article, produce a package or post some information. Always remember you aren't writing for yourself – you are writing for the readers.

Don't write 1,000 words when 500 will do. Don't use words you wouldn't normally use because you got a "word-a-day" calendar for your birthday. Don't drag people through twists and turns when a straight line is a better way to get from Point A to Point B. Overwritten, meandering stories likely bother you to the point of distraction. If that's true, don't write that way.

This maxim goes beyond the text portion of the field and can be applied to any of the tools you use in convergent journalism. Video stories on the Web, for example, are just as guilty of violating this rule as print stories are. When you post a video online, you are asking your audience members to shift from an active media experience to a passive one. This means you must give them a good reason to stop hopping from site to site and watch your video.

Would you watch a 15-minute video of your university president, standing at a podium, mumbling something about how students are a "vital resource" on your campus? Probably not, so think long and hard about why you would want to post video in that format. In some cases, some of your more "news junkie" audience members might really want to see the video in its entirety. In these cases, you can consider posting the whole video. However, if it's clear to you that no one would really get anything out of this, cut a few key soundbites from the video and post them with some text-based information to introduce them.

Go through your photo slideshows with the same sense of purpose. Just because you can empty your camera's memory card into a slideshow, it doesn't mean you should. Instead, eliminate things that you wouldn't want to see as a viewer. Remove photos that don't add to the overall story and delete images that are repetitive. This will lead to a tighter story and a grateful audience.

Right tool, right job

Storytelling isn't just about writing, shooting or drawing. It's about making your point in the clearest possible way. Photographers often say "A picture is worth a thousand words," which is true when you are capturing scenery or emotional exchanges among people. In other cases, a thousand words could run circles around a photo, especially when the photo is just someone standing at a podium.

In convergent journalism, storytelling is about using the best tool to accomplish the job. People erroneously assume that convergence is all about making things digital or using video. Instead, this approach to storytelling is about making sure that people get the best story in the most appropriate format.

Consider how best to give your readers the story. In some cases, text works beautifully while in other cases a graphic will be a much better option. Photos can do things that video can't and the opposite is also true. Examine each tool and figure out what benefits it can provide to your readers as you approach each storytelling opportunity.

Show, don't tell

Writers often can't seem to get out of their own way during a story. They want to tell you that something is "the most important issue" or that someone is "extremely fortunate," and in doing so, they violate one of the primary rules of storytelling: Show, don't tell.

Showing is the way to really explain a story. Don't tell me, "Here is a rich man." Instead, show me the facts that support your point. The man drives a new car each week and gives away the old one to charity. He owns a home in all 50 states so he doesn't have to worry about finding a hotel room when he travels. Countries who can't get financial support from China reach out to him for help. Those facts would have any reader saying, "Wow! This guy is rich!"

If you let the sources and the facts do the hard work for you, the storytelling becomes much easier. In addition, the readers will come to the conclusions on their own and be much more satisfied with what they learn.

VIEW FROM A PRO

HOLLY HEYSER

Holly Heyser has covered everything from lame-duck governors in Virginia to duck-hunting excursions in California. In between, she worked as a business reporter and editor, served as an adviser for a college newspaper and took up food photography. In each phase of her career, Heyser has focused on how best to tell stories to her audience.

Figure 5.1
Holly Heyser.

"When I covered state legislatures, I had to be fluent in the language of politics, but to write stories, I had to translate for consumers – the group of people affected by any particular story. Easy to say, hard to do," she said. "Where the need to understand your audience became crystal clear for me was my return to the student newspaper as faculty adviser. . . . I finally started saying, 'Write stories YOU would want to read, not what you think your professors or the administration would want to read,' and they turned out some great stuff."

In her current job as the editor of California Waterfowl Magazine, she said she is using every skill she has picked up over her entire career to tell stories. In doing so, she noted that she always keeps an eye on her readers and what they would want to see.

"How you figure out your audience isn't rocket science," Heyser said. "First, who reads your publication? When I worked for the Orange County Register, I knew my audience tilted heavily conservative and not obsessed with public affairs. At the [St. Paul, Minnesota] Pioneer Press, it was fairly liberal and deeply interested in public affairs. At the magazine I run now, my audience is pretty much entirely duck hunters. But that knowledge just gives you broad parameters. For each story, you need to think about who might want to read it and whom you think needs to read it. Now, what stuff that you found interesting during reporting would appeal to THAT audience? There's your story."

Heyser said she became more comfortable with this approach once she started her hunting blog, where her audience's feedback helped shape her topic selection and story approach. She said she learned that writing is about clear communication, not following overly strict rules.

"All too often [students] try to write the way they think they're supposed to write, which is all too often boring," she said. "Even when I was in school back in the 80s, I knew 'boring' was the kiss of death for a story. People's attention spans are WAY shorter now, so boring is even worse."

Although she knows storytelling takes time and talent, she said it isn't beyond the reach of anyone who really wants to do it.

"We have been storytellers since we've had language – *we know how to do this.* Trust yourself," Heyser said. "Take any story you like – and by 'story' I mean a story in *any* form, including video, comedy or Facebook posts – and think about why it engages you. Emulate that. It might feel like copying, but repeat it often enough and you will discover your own touches that make your writing very *you*, and you might even do something completely new, a game-changer in storytelling. Man, that feels *so good*. And it's totally doable."

Structuring Your Stories

The idea behind structure is to give your readers a clear path through a story. Whether the story is a hard-hitting investigative report on financial mismanagement or a child's bedtime book, the writer has to look for ways to present information in a clear and coherent format. For convergent journalists, the pattern of storytelling will deviate slightly as they operate across different media platforms. However, every story should have three basic things: a beginning, a middle and an end.

Beginning: Make me care

Audiences have more choices than ever before when it comes to what media they will read, watch or otherwise consume. The days of a handful of TV stations, a newspaper and a few magazines have been replaced by thousands of channels and millions of websites. Through each of these media outlets, an almost unlimited amount of content pours forth, forcing readers to make quicker decisions regarding what they will and will not spend time with.

This makes the beginning of your story more important than ever before. If you only get a fraction of a moment to capture the attention of a reader, you need to put your best foot forward in hopes of doing so. This is where strong starts can benefit you as a storyteller.

Hard leads

In traditional media terms, the opening of a story is called a lead and it is meant to provide the reader with the most important information on a given topic. We usually refer to this as the 5Ws and 1H, or the "who," "what," "when," "where," "why" and "how" of a story. This approach is direct and it gives you the best chance to grab your readers right away. If you don't provide this material immediately, you can distract or annoy your readers.

67

When it comes to hard news, the audience members want to know how bad a fire was, who won a game or what a new law means to them. They don't care which fire department responded to the fire, how long the game took or if two city council members were sniping at one another.

Here's an example of what we mean: Imagine you go home today after class and your roommate says to you, "Hey, your mom called. There was a fire at her house." What would be the *first* thing you would want to know? You would probably ask if anyone was hurt. You might then ask how big the fire was or how much damage it did. You probably would want to know how the fire started. Instead of telling you any of this information, however, your roommate started off with "The Johnson County Fire Department responded to a fire at 111 W. Main St. Ladder truck 11, chief 12 and pump truck 18 responded along with members of Fire House 28 . . . " At a certain point, you will probably start yelling at your roommate, "JUST TELL ME WHAT HAPPENED!"

Put yourself in the place of the readers when you are writing. Just tell them what happened.

Soft leads

Not all stories are meant to have a lead that gives the readers a quick, punchy look at the news. In many cases, a short observation, a decent anecdote or a narrative opening can provide your readers with a much better reason to read on.

If you are writing longer stories, such as personality profiles or in-depth pieces, you can rely on a softer lead to help people see an issue from a different perspective or a more emotional angle.

For example, a story about a baseball player at your university who broke his leg during a game, spent six months rehabilitating his injury and then led his team to the College World Series has the makings of a compelling story. However, if you write a lead that simply lays out those facts in a way similar to what you see above, you won't get many readers to emotionally invest in this story.

A story that begins with a description can get the reader's attention better:

> Bobby Smith took his lead off first base, dancing back and forth between safety and danger, hoping to distract the pitcher. It was the first practice of the season, but for Smith, every minute on the diamond was a minute spent perfecting his craft.

The lanky lefty on the mound ignored Smith and delivered a curveball to the plate, inducing batter John Witzmar to slap a tailor-made double-play ball to the shortstop.

"The minute he hit the ball," Smith said, recalling the event almost a year later, "I could hear my dad hollering in my head, 'Hustle! Hustle!' I had to break up the double play."

Smith's spikes dug into the semi-frozen infield and tore up chunks of dirt as he flew toward second. He was out by a country mile, but he could still protect Witzmar if he could just get to second fast enough.

"It was a clean play," Smith said. "I went in low and I slid hard. My foot hit the bag and our second baseman, Carlos, went up in the air to avoid me. Then, everything went wrong."

A sickening crack sliced through the infield chatter as Smith hit the bag. Doctors would later diagnose it as a compound fracture of the tibia. The bone pressed outward against his skin and pain tore through him as if he had been shot.

"My sock was distorted, the way the bone had stuck out," he said. "I tried to stand up but nothing moved. For the first time in my life, I thought, 'Oh, God. I might never play again.'"

As Smith told the story of his gruesome injury, he gestured to his mended leg with a hand that sported a College World Series championship ring. From the grim diagnosis, to his yearlong rehab and through to his MVP performance in the World Series, Smith said he clung to the word he heard in his head the day of his injury: Hustle.

The soft lead brings the readers into the scene at the very moment in which the player broke his leg. In doing so, the readers are allowed to feel sympathy for him and also follow him through his journey into recovery and through to redemption. However, notice how the soft lead ends on a hard bit of information: Who he is and why we should care about him. This element, which follows the pattern of an inverted pyramid lead, is called a nut paragraph and allows for you to seal off the narrative lead and move the reader into the meat of the story.

Middle: Make it matter

Once you grab your readers' attention, you need to keep it. In terms of writing, graphics, videos or slideshows, the core of the piece is where the most important material resides. Each paragraph, each second and each image in the middle of your story is another opportunity for you to retain your audience members or lose them. This is why you have to make your middle matter.

Here are several key things to consider when shaping the middle of your story.

Value

In print journalism, reporters often discuss a concept called "notebook emptying." The idea behind it is that reporters feel that if they gathered information, they don't want it to go to waste. Thus, they shake every fact, quote and anecdote out of their notebooks and put them in the story. This approach can lead to bloated stories that contain large chunks of material lacking in value.

Value should be at the forefront of your mind in everything you do, but it is particularly important in the middle. After you write your lead, find your establishing shot or in some other way actively engage the audience, you might find yourself relaxing a bit too much in your work. It's often a chore to find the most important information or craft that perfect lead, so once you get past it, you probably feel ready for a break. However, when you build the middle of your story, keep providing your readers with value. The minute you stop doing this is the minute they give up and move on to something else.

When you build your piece, each paragraph needs to reinforce the lead. When you are creating a video story, each shot should give the readers a reason to stay engaged. When you put together a slide show, each image must tell a story and advance the overall storytelling goals of the slideshow.

Repetition

In some instances of storytelling, repetition has its place. In video, the repeating of a soundbite, a video clip or natural sound can provide impact and value as the journalist attempts to show consistency. In print, repetition can provide cadence for the readers, giving them the sense that a fact is crucial to the overall story.

However, in many cases, repetition isn't part of a larger storytelling approach. Instead, it is simply journalists not being careful.

When you go through a story, look for the big cases of repetition, such as paraphrases and quotes that say the same thing or sources who repeat themselves for no reason. Eliminate these major repetitions and then focus on the minor repetitions as well. When you have four adjectives in a sentence, try to eliminate three of them. When you have someone who provides you with quotes that fail to gain traction in storytelling, condense the bloated quote into a stronger chunk of paraphrase. When you find yourself using redundant phrases like "completely destroyed" or "armed gunman," remove them and make your writing leaner.

In photography, examine the images in the middle of your photo story to see if you have too many shots of a single subject. If you do, pick the one or two that best convey your message and cut the rest.

Boredom

This goes back to the first rule we mentioned in this chapter: If you wouldn't read it, don't write it. The same basic concept applies to video, audio, photography and graphics. Just because you get excited about writing 10,000 words on public policy or producing a 20-minute video on a soccer match, it doesn't follow that your audience members will want to stick around for every word or every second of your story.

The human attention span is only a few seconds long. Every few moments, you have to poke people to keep them alert and attentive. With this in mind, you have to take a "seek and destroy" approach as you review the middle of your story for boring material. Take the opportunity here to switch from reporter to editor and look for things that shouldn't be there.

71

End: Find closure

Anyone who has watched an old Western movie knows how these pieces of Americana traditionally end: The good guy vanquishes the bad guy, he gets the girl and they ride off together into the sunset as the credits roll. This approach gives the audience no sense of ambiguity. The movie is over.

Stories you tell have a similar need, a sense of closure. However, you can't just slap "The End" on the piece after your final paragraph or last image. You have to find a way to seal off the story and give readers a feeling of finality.

Text

In text writing, a good closing quote will usually do the trick. As you do your interviews for a story, you can look for something one of your sources says that provides you with a good ending. This could be a city council representative saying, "The meeting might be over, but this issue is far from resolved." Quotes like this allow you to demonstrate that the piece is finished without you as the writer having to say it. When you insert yourself into the end of a story, the closing can feel like you are telling people "the moral of the story is . . . " Let the source do the heavy lifting for you.

If you don't want to rely on a quote, a simple summary of fact could help you here as well. To close a preview to a meeting, you could note, "The Jackson County School Board will review this issue in its March 4 meeting." This is a fact, so you don't end up doing a morality play, and yet you can still close the story.

Video

In broadcast, journalists have the ability to end their pieces in a number of ways that will bring the story to a close. One of the more traditional ways of ending a broadcast package (see Chapter 8) is with the reporter wrapping things up in a stand-up. The reporter will summarize the story before signing off with his or her name and the station's call letters. This clearly shows the viewers that the reporter has completed the task at hand and the newscast is ready to move on.

In other cases, the reporter would be live on the set or live on the scene of an event. This would allow the package to end with a closing shot or a closing soundbite before the journalist comes back on screen to do a short question and answer session with the anchor. At the end of this, the anchor usually thanks the reporter and the newscast moves on.

For videos on the Web, where this interaction isn't necessary, the journalist's wrap-up described above would usually work best, with the reporter signing off on the story either with a voice-over or stand-up presentation.

STRUCTURE FORMATS

Here are a few types of structure you can consider:

- Inverted pyramid: This is the traditional format of print and online news stories. The goal of this format is to provide the 5Ws and 1H as high as possible in your story and then build the remaining parts of the story in descending order of importance. Each paragraph after the lead should be less important than the lead, but should also aid the lead in telling the story. Paragraphs at the bottom of the story are less important than those closer to the top.

- Narrative: This format tends to work well in broadcast, as it is both simple and clear. In most cases, people have become accustomed to a narrative approach and it therefore makes it easy to consume in both an aural and visual approach.

In this approach to storytelling, journalists give a strong account of events through the use of characters and actions. (The soft lead above is a good example of this.) The piece is balanced through the positions each source takes within the story and then concludes, even if the news itself isn't over. An example of this would be a broadcast report of a school board meeting in which the board members are discussing the value of adding technology to a particular school in the district. Some members will support the idea, making a case that technology will improve the lives of the students. Others will argue against it, noting that the costs are too high or that the board can't play favorites among the schools in the district. In the end, the board will either vote on the issue (resolution) or push the decision off to another meeting (conclusion). In either case, the story ends.

- Hourglass: This format requires you to blend both of the aforementioned stories into a single approach to storytelling. An hourglass format requires the writer to sum up the core of the story in about five or six paragraphs in an inverted-pyramid fashion. After that, the story takes a turn, providing the readers with a short transition that allows them to see that the story will now continue in a different way. The story then moves into a narrative format in which the piece has a beginning, a middle and an end, where the writer weaves together chronology, quotes and other elements to tell a richer and deeper story.

- Circular/chronological: In some broadcast news stories, journalists employ a more "circular" approach to the story, which uses chronology as well as some elements of an inverted pyramid to tell a story. The stories traditionally start with a lead that more directly mimics a newspaper headline. Since broadcast journalism uses passive media, people often divide their attention among several tasks while the news is on. To make sure the viewers and listeners are attuned to a story that has value to them, the lead must get their attention without giving away too much. You can think of the lead the way you would consider starting a conversation: "Hey, did you hear about X?" This will allow the audience members to adjust their attention to the story and then you can begin with the core of the piece.

The story will then develop in chronological order until it leads all the way back to the beginning. For example, a crime story could lead with, "Police are looking for a man who robbed the Quik-E-Mart on Smith Street tonight." The story would then settle into the chronology of the event: the man entered around 8 p.m., displayed a handgun and demanded money. He then fled on foot toward Main Street. After the chronology, the story bends back toward the beginning with a description of the suspect and a plea to the public: "Anyone who has seen this man is asked to contact the police department at 555–1212." This brings the story back around to the beginning element where the journalist noted police were looking for the man.

FINAL FOUR

If you take nothing else away from this chapter, here are four things you should remember:

1 Work for your audience. Don't write for the sake of writing or because you think you matter. Don't throw together a ton of photos and figure the audience members will figure out what to do with them. Don't run an overly long video just because you didn't want to cut any of it. You need to build your stories for the purpose of satisfying your audience members. If you wouldn't want to read it, see it or listen to it, don't publish it.

2 Structure matters in storytelling. Great stories are said to "tell themselves." That misperception has led to some horrible storytelling. Don't think that you can put the pieces of a story together any which way and things will be fine. Determine how best to order the elements of your stories and then present them accordingly. If the pieces are well-structured, they will come across clearly and smoothly.

3 Use the best tool to tell your stories. Not every tool is equal when it comes to storytelling. As a convergent journalist, your job is to figure out which approach will give your audience members the most bang for their buck. Don't gravitate toward a single tool because it is the one with which you feel the most comfort. Consider text, photos, audio, video and graphics as your potential storytelling tools and then apply the best one in each situation.

4 Storytelling is natural. As Holly Heyser said, storytelling is something people have been doing forever. Focus on what matters most, convey your message in a clear and coherent fashion and give your readers a sense of value based on what you've given to them. You can do this.

Photography 6

Timothy R. Gleason

Introduction

A camera is an amazing piece of engineering because whether it costs $5,000 or $100, it is still a box with a hole that lets in light. Cameras are produced for a variety of purposes, yet they all do the same basic thing: Record an image of the scene in front of them.

The aim of this chapter is to help you learn enough about photography so you can make the kind of photographs you envision. This chapter reviews the technical aspects of cameras, introduces you to image composition and advises you on how to use this knowledge to tell stories visually. This chapter will combine both a basic-level walkthrough of photography as well as a higher-level approach to some more complex photography terms. As with any aspect of this book, some of this will be more valuable to you if you are interested in this specific area of convergence. However, even if you see yourself as being more of a graphic or text reporter, understanding how photography works can benefit you as you converse with photo journalists and plan your overall approach to storytelling.

Cameras and How They Work

Before you can get the best images out of a camera, you need to understand how a camera works. The word photography means writing with light, and cameras do just that by capturing the light reflecting off objects to create images. Accepting this fact enables you to understand why your photographs have turned out a certain way. For example, you might notice that a great-looking sunset behind your friend turned this person into a silhouette. That's because there is more light coming toward the camera from the sun that there is reflecting off the subject's face.

Inside the Lens

The most underrated part of the camera is the lens, which reshapes the light coming into the camera. The camera's lens is actually a family of elements, which may be composed of glass or plastic. The lens is able to focus and magnify light through the movement of the lens elements in relation to each other, thereby focusing light on the surface of a sensor. Budding photographers must realize the limitations of the lens as well as the other parts of the camera and then align their expectations with the equipment.

Apertures

After passing through the lens' front elements, the light goes through the aperture, which is the hole in the lens that allows a certain amount of light through. The aperture is located in the rear part of the lens. Photographers adjust the aperture to maximize or minimize the amount of light entering the camera. The aperture also affects the range of sharpness. Setting the aperture to its smallest f-stop number equates to "opening the lens" to a '"wider aperture," in photo slang, to allow in more light. So as the hole gets larger to allow in more light, less depth of field is achieved. As the hole becomes smaller, more depth of field results. Opening the aperture reduces depth of field for a smaller range of sharpness, and stopping down increases the range of sharpness. You now have the power to do something with your camera that you can't do with your eyes – make objects at different distances vary in sharpness.

F-stop numbers

F-stop numbers represent the size of an aperture's opening. Small-numbered f-stops represent larger openings than big-numbered f-stops. This seemingly illogical relationship confounds many people new to photography, who don't know that an f-stop is the product of dividing the length of the lens (front element to back element) by the diameter of the aperture opening. Most lenses have a range of f-stops that can be changed by the user or the camera's programming. If a lens ranges from f2 to f22, this means f2 allows in the most light while f22 allows in the least light. Furthermore, f2 produces the least depth of field while f22 provides the most depth of field. The range of f-stops will vary from lens to lens.

Figure 6.1 *This graphic of a lens shows various aperture settings that let in varying amounts of light.*

(SOURCE: MIRJANAJOVIC/ISTOCK VECTORS/GETTY IMAGES)

Inside the Camera Body

After the light has moved through the lens elements and aperture, it needs to reach the recording surface. Some cameras use a mirror to reflect incoming light to a viewfinder made of a prism or mirror.

The most common type of camera using a mirror is the single-lens reflex (SLR, or DSLR for the digital version). The mirror enables the user to see the scene by looking into the optical viewfinder. Because the light moves through the lens, up from the mirror and into the optical viewfinder, users get to quickly see the image with clarity.

Almost every DSLR moves the mirror upward, causing a momentary blackout effect as light passes underneath the mirror, so the light can pass under the mirror and to the sensor. The rapid movement of the mirror causes a problem known as camera shake, which can contribute to pictures being blurry. Camera designers have resolved some of the problems with new "mirrorless" designs that send an electronic signal to the window on the back of the camera, known as a live view on the DSLR. Although the mirrorless designs allow for quieter picture taking and smaller camera bodies, the electronic viewfinders tend to suffer from a lag not present with optical viewfinders.

Shutter vibration and sound

With or without a mirror, the light needs to hit the sensor. Two kinds of shutters allow the pixels of the sensor to receive the light. The traditional kind is the mechanical shutter of a focal plane type, which involves moving two metal shutters out of the way and putting them back in place. Photographers often prefer quieter picture taking because it allows them to work more stealthily. Some cameras allow

78

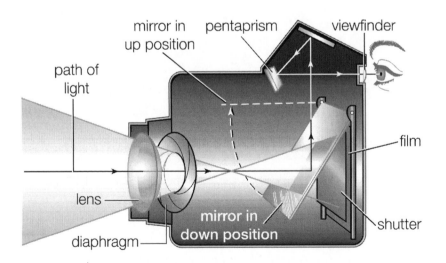

Figure 6.2 *Camera body with labeled parts.*
(SOURCE: ENCYCLOPAEDIA BRITANNICA/UNIVERSAL IMAGES GROUP/GETTY IMAGES)

users to choose the volume and sound of the shutter, in order to allow for both quiet photography and a more traditional experience.

The shutter can remain can remain "open" longer to allow in more light or shorter to freeze action. The problem with "slower" shutter speeds is that movement, either by the subject or the photographer, results in blurry pictures. Because "faster" shutter speeds freeze action, those like 1/250, 1/500 and 1/1000 are used to accurately capture the moments of action. Slower shutter speeds, such as 1/125, 1/60 and 1/30 are best for non-moving subjects or to intentionally show action as a blur, and they frequently require a tripod.

Choosing the Right Tool for the Job

Anyone, professional or amateur, needs to understand how a camera works to be able to choose the right camera for the subject. Sometimes, the ever-so-convenient cell phone will do the job, but other times only a professional DSLR will suffice.

The cell/mobile phone camera

The mobile phone has revolutionized photography because, for many people, it is a ubiquitous tool. There is a popular saying: "The best camera is the one you have with you." For now, the cell phone camera has significant limitations. These limitations include the following issues:

- While the regular zoom lens is an optical zoom – meaning the optics physically move to zoom in and out – the cell phone uses a digital zoom, which crops and enlarges the image. The resulting photograph does not have the same image quality as one made with an optical zoom.
- If you want your subject to fill your frame, the cell phone user must be close to the subject. Your feet become your zoom lens.
- Regular cameras take pictures first and foremost, and are usually not useful for sending images. Smart cell phones do all sorts of things, so the camera is not a priority, thus leading to weaker images.

The quality of mobile phone cameras will continue to improve, although they will remain inferior in image quality to cameras with larger sensors. For now, the mobile phone camera will suffice for still shots of people under good lighting and well-lit landscapes where fine detail hardly matters.

Compact camera

The compact camera market is dying from cell phone popularity. As the sensors in cell phone cameras improve in size, pixel count and programming, the compact camera's superior qualities are reduced and become less significant. One of the few advantages of the compact camera compared to the cell phone is its lens, which is typically an optical zoom lens that produces a superior image. Cell phone users have to move to make their subject larger or smaller, while people with regular cameras can zoom in or out.

Furthermore, many compact cameras are easier to hold than cell phones. Better ergonomics enable camera users to make pictures without the blurriness caused by camera shake. Compact cameras also

CHOOSING THE RIGHT TOOL FOR THE JOB

The table below represents the characteristics of different categories of cameras. Some categories may have a wide range of levels of camera.

	Cell phone	Compact	Mirrorless system	DSLR system
Types	Camera built into phone; tend to have similar options	Lenses cannot be changed; almost all models are cheapest in price	Most models are at advanced consumer to enthusiast level, but professional models have emerged	Inexpensive camera body and one lens kits typically start around $500; professional model bodies cost thousands of dollars
Portability	Easy	Convenient	Convenient to somewhat inconvenient	Inconvenient
Best uses	Unexpected moments; subtle photographs; well-lit scenes	Family gatherings when a cell phone isn't good enough	Travel and walk-around photography	Difficult subjects, like motion and bad lighting
Best outputs	Mobile devices, and small and medium screens	Mobile devices, most screens and small prints	From screen to finer printing	From screen to finer printing

tend to have more manual control options than cell phone cameras for greater creative control.

Mirrorless and DSLR systems

Two camera designs are popular with advanced amateurs and professionals: mirrorless and DSLR systems. These systems allow for interchangeable lenses, which are typically of higher quality than built-in lenses. Because of their larger sensors, better lens options and quicker operating functions, the mirrorless and DSLR interchangeable-lens systems are the preferred choices for professional work.

Most mirrorless and DSLR systems are popular because of their sensors' sensitivity ratings, or the light-absorbing properties of the sensor. Sensitivity is identified by the ISO, for International Organization for Standardization, and is represented by numbers. The higher the ISO number the less light you will need to capture the image. Higher numbers also increase the risk of image degradation through color distortion and reduced sharpness.

Each individual sensor produces a picture element known as a pixel. Having more pixels enables larger printing but not necessarily better-looking images. Take a 10-megapixel camera, for example.

81

ISO	≤ 200	200–400	400–800	Above 800
Detail/ color	Best	Slight decline in quality visible	Continual slight decline in better cameras, but cell phones and compacts show significant decline	Loss of quality becomes more noticeable with higher ISOs and smaller sensors
Uses	Sunny days; studio photography	Action on sunny or slightly overcast day	Action with darker outdoor lighting; well-lit indoor scenes without action	Low-lighting with people when tripod can't be used, people moving
Cameras	All work best in this range	Decline least visible in larger sensor cameras, like DSLR and mirrorless; may be top of range for many cell phone and compact cameras	Reproduction with cell phones and compacts will show significant visual noise (loss of detail, color inaccuracies in shadows)	The best DSLR and mirrorless cameras show significant superiority; cell phones and compacts shouldn't be used unless no other camera is available

This camera would have a 10-million-pixel sensor, which is really 10 million individual sensors working together.

There is no perfect camera because certain situations call for specific cameras. It is important to understand the basic principles of photography and the various camera functions to determine which camera you need. While the photographer's vision is more important than the camera, a picture can't be made without one.

The Photographer's Vision

Photographers organize various objects within a frame when they construct images. Photographers use various visual composition skills to make mundane subjects appear more interesting.

Design basics

Before getting into framing, it is helpful to understand some fundamental design principles. Everyone knows what a "line" is, but not everyone knows that different lines communicate different ideas. A horizontal line across the frame is familiar and reassuring because it resembles the horizon we are all familiar with. For example, it is reassuring to walk along an even and flat floor, but it is not reassuring to walk across a jagged and angled floor. As a line appears thinner, the line communicates more lightness, airiness, delicateness and softness than a thicker line. As a line becomes thicker, it also becomes more solid and almost trustworthy.

Vertical lines are more dynamic than horizontal lines because they run perpendicular to the reassuring horizontal lines. Vertical lines are also commonplace in our environments, yet they are not as reassuring as horizontal lines because they move up and down while we tend to look left and right.

A diagonal line would seem to be the average of the two and feel moderately reassuring. However, diagonal lines are considered action lines because they suggest movement and following them forces us to look both across and up through a plane. Photographers and other visual communicators use diagonal lines to create excitement, motion and drama. Use caution when emphasizing diagonal lines. In most cases, they should appear naturally in the environment, such as a railroad crossing sign or the Y-intersection road sign. Avoid tilting the camera at an angle to force diagonal lines. As Tom Ang noted in "Picture Editing", the horizontal and vertical lines of subjects should usually run parallel to the sides of pictures.

Figure 6.3 *This image demonstrates the power of lines to give weight – the thick black lines – and to give direction, because the repeating, thick lines move your eyes from the right/front to the left/back.*

Faces

Photography frequently involves faces, especially journalistic photography. People read newspapers, magazines and websites and people have a tendency to be drawn to other people. Trees, puppies and kittens do not consume media, so photojournalists should use them sparingly. The most dramatic way to represent a face is to show it straight on or in profile. The angled face may have become popular because it shows both sides but emphasizes a so-called "better side," yet this perspective is not as dramatic as the alternatives. Expressions also matter to photographers, who may look at hundreds of frames of a subject, looking for just the right appearance.

In addition, facial features often allow photographers to showcase emotion and feeling while capturing key moments in events. For example, a photo of a player who has just scored a game-winning touchdown will have more value if that player's face is prominent in the shot. The smile, the tears of joy and the expression of satisfaction

84

Figure 6.4 *The photograph of this young man conveys value through the accentuation of his facial features, which clearly denote his displeasure.*

(COURTESY OF MELISSA BEYER)

Figure 6.5 *This image demonstrates the principles of repetition of pattern and branches' weighty lines as strength. Images can contain more than one principle as this one does. Notice how the snow-covered bird's nest breaks up the repetition of pattern and its roundness contrasts against the heavy lines.*

all convey the elation of the moment. Conversely, a player who just lost the game on that same touchdown will also showcase emotion within the moment. The sadness on that player's face can tell a story just as easily and as powerfully.

Patterns

Many visual communicators use repetition to increase interest in a picture. This practice shows the same or similar objects multiple times in a photograph. Repetition can be found in the hurdles during a track meet, students standing in line buying books and the rows of desks in a classroom. A photographer or designer will often provide some element that stands out from this repetition, however. Maybe a runner has tripped over a hurdle while the rest of the racers clear them or one shopper is falling asleep in the checkout line or a student sits at a desk looking befuddled.

VIEW FROM A PRO

MELISSA LYTTLE

Melissa Lyttle is a photojournalist on the "Enterprise Team" of the Tampa Bay Times, which produces a monthly narrative journalism magazine. This affords her the opportunity to spend more time with her subjects and colleagues than most photojournalists can when working for daily newspapers.

"I always try to find out everything I can about the story or subject beforehand, and have a conversation with the subject if possible before making a picture, so I can do the best job of putting myself in the right place at the right time," she said. "And then I'm usually on the road, trying to spend as much quality time on the assignment as possible before publication."

Figure 6.6
Melissa Lyttle.

The magazine's team approach requires more collaboration than many other photojournalists have with their colleagues.

"A typical week for me right now consists of a budget meeting on Monday, planning out the week with the team of writers I'm assigned to," Lyttle said. "We all bring story ideas to this pitch meeting and bounce things off of each other before they're fully formed to get feedback and help shaping the idea. The rest of the week I'm usually in research mode or photography mode."

Lyttle said she didn't jump straight into magazine teamwork. She studied journalism in college and she had four internships, including one at her current employer. She was employed at the Fort Lauderdale Sun-Sentinel for five years before rejoining the Times.

She said practice has been the key to helping her hone her photography skills at each stage of her career.

"The only way you're going to get better at anything is by doing it," she said. "Plain and simple. If you want to get better at photographing news, listen to a police scanner and send yourself out to cover things."

Even though subjects differ, Lyttle said she approaches scenes by looking for three things: "Moment, light and composition – always," she said.

She said beginning photographers should work on the basics to improve their craft. Fundamentally, they need to learn to make sharp photographs by focusing on the simple things.

"As simple as this sounds, it's probably focus and a steady hand," she said. "I've seen way too many blurry, unusable photos from photographers just learning."

STABILITY

The ability to keep the camera steady is one of the toughest things for beginning photographers. Here are several suggestions to help you improve stability:

- Lean on something: Find a stationary object that will help you keep your body stable. This object can be anything from a tree to a wall, as long as it is sturdy and will prevent you from wobbling.

- Lower your center of gravity: Although this can change your perspective, you can squat down into a crouch or sit on the ground to help you become more stable.

- Use a stabilizing device: Tripods and monopods are great tools to help keep your camera stable. In addition, other everyday items can become stabilizing devices. You can set your camera on a table or a chair. If you are concerned about the camera sliding around, invest in a beanbag and place the camera on that.

- Focus on your breathing: If you are panicking about the shoot or if the adrenaline is running high for you, you will likely twitch and thus create blurry or unstable photos. Focus on slowing your breathing and depress your shutter when you exhale.

Color and Grayscale

Photographers must also contend with the issues of color and grayscale when making and editing photographs. Certain colors attract more attention than others, and some photographers look for bold colors in scenes. Photographers refer to images that stand out for their color or grayscale contrast as ones that "pop."

A color image that pops has many bright, bold colors or one or two colors that jump from plainer surroundings. An image of a field of tulips pops if well lit by the sun, as does a red barn against a blue sky. Naturally occurring images can pop, but the intensity and direction of the light can make it challenging for photographers working to a deadline. Some photographers use shortcuts like Instagram or Adobe Photoshop to saturate their images for attention, but these tend to look unrealistic. Additionally, news organizations frown on the significant alteration of images because the images no longer represent the reality of the scene.

Figure 6.7 *The red of the traditional British telephone booth and the bright green of the foliage create an image that leads to a great color pop. See the color image on the companion site at: www.focalpress.com/cw/filak.*

Figure 6.8 *In the color version of this image, shown on the companion website, you can see how the photographer captured the ambient color produced by the lights, thus also capturing the mood of a big city at night. www.focalpress.com/cw/filak, for the color figure.*

Light as color

The color of light can also create a mood, so photographers use the ambient light (light in the environment) to communicate the essence of a place. Photographers often manually set the color balance on their cameras so the camera doesn't compensate for the color of the light. A dreary office is enhanced by showing the green from the fluorescent lights; two people holding hands on the beach look better against the yellow-red light of a sunset; and the bluish noon sunlight makes the devilish downward shadows look even more unfriendly. Consider the color of light before leaving the camera on auto white-balance. The color of the light can help to tell the story, too

The ambient color produced by the street and car lights in Figure 6.8 result in a color effect that appears somewhat unnatural, yet also authentic to anyone who has been out at night in a big city. If the photographer had used an auto white-balance approach to compensate for the color, the scene might feel less authentic. The effect is similar to that of an incandescent light bulb, which produces a warmish yellow color compared to midday light. That light may not appear natural compared to neutral daylight, but getting rid of that color in a photo makes a warm indoor scene look like it was taken outdoors.

Old-school pop

Grayscale images, popularly known as black and white, can pop because of their contrast, which is the range of tones between black and white in an image. High-contrast images have fewer tones but pronounced darker and lighter tones, while low-contrast images have pronounced gray tones in the middle section of the grayscale. Images with a slight increase in contrast can offer a more realistic image, still with some pop.

Whether you want color or grayscale pop, muted tones or realism, you can change the settings in the camera to produce these effects. Some cameras have menu options to show scenes with saturation or with muted colors. Depending on the make and model of the camera, this option can be found under color mode or art filters. If you are working for online publication and not print, you will want your camera to produce Red-Green-Blue (RGB) images, not Cyan-Magenta-Yellow-Black (CMYK). Properly setting the camera options will help to provide the color representation you want.

SHOWING TEXTURE

One of the toughest aspects for photographers is showing a subject's texture. Visible texture enhances the appearance of reality because the photograph seems to be more lifelike. Most objects, like wood, grains and metal, require sharp representation to show their textures. The focus has to be precise when the texture needs to stand out. Photographers can improve their chances of locking in the focus if they use a tripod and a deeper depth of field.

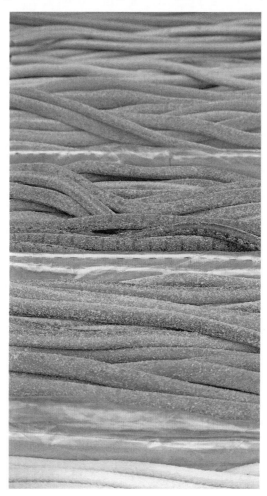

Figure 6.9 *See the companion website, www.focalpress.com/cw/filak, for the color figure of the candy ropes.*

Notice how the candy ropes appearing sharpest also reveal the most texture, thus also feeling more realistic. While all the ropes are covered in sugar, the ones in focus appear to have more sugar because their texture is more visible.

Framing

The over-reliance on centering is one of the worst forms of redundancy in photography, second only to parents who tell their children to smile for the camera. This is not to suggest a subject should never be centered. An example of centering frequently seen in the press is the mug shot. This head-and-shoulders shot has equivalent space around the head to the frame, with the exception of the greater space under the chin. While the head is not perfectly centered, its close positioning to the center demonstrates the limited value of this composition.

A centered subject has the ability to draw attention to it because of the habit of the viewer to look in the middle. A centered composition also tends to be symmetrical in design, so the picture looks balanced.

A way to simplify the composition is to exclude other visual elements, either by not having other details around or using a telephoto lens. The subject takes over the frame through its isolation from the rest of the visual world. If you want your single subject to command attention, don't place any other details in the frame. In contrast, the scaling of visual elements emphasizes a centered subject by making it larger than the other visual elements. Photographers will get closer to the subject to make it appear larger than other things in the frame, which makes the subject appear more important.

A wide-angle lens, for example, inherently represents reality but is often perceived as a distortion. Whatever is closest to the lens becomes larger, and objects quickly become smaller in the distance. This is sort of like the effect of holding a pencil up to your face while also seeing the skyscraper in the background. They look to be the same size, but you know your pencil is not as large as a skyscraper because your mind rationalizes the relationship. Some photographers center their subjects in the frame with the wide-angle lens by getting close to the subject, which emphasizes the subject and reduces the size of the background elements. The background may appear sharp because of the depth of field, however. For example, some photographs of a singer will place that person in front with the band members smaller in the background.

Figure 6.10 *This is an example showing how centering is not necessarily boring. All the lines lead you to the man in the alley, but the photo is not just about him. Otherwise, he'd be too small.*

93

Playing by the Rule of Thirds

A more popular way to compose is to apply the Rule of Thirds, which isn't so much a rule as it is a highly recommended asymmetrical composition. Some cameras and image-editing programs are making it easy to crop images following the Rule of Thirds by applying a simple 3-by-3 grid over the image. By cutting up the frame with two equally spaced horizontal lines and two equally spaced vertical lines, the frame is now divided into kind of a tic-tac-toe board. The Rule of Thirds requires the photographer to place the main element at the intersection of the lines. Imagine photographing a housing developer while trying to show the land and the emerging homes. A poorly composed photograph would place the developer in the center next to a house that dwarfs the person. A better composition would place the developer along one of the vertical lines with the head at the top intersection. Filling the rest of the frame is the landscape of emerging homes. This composition allows the viewer to see the human subject easily, as well as the housing development that is the reason for the story.

Figure 6.11 *Image-editing software, like Adobe Photoshop, will allow you to view your images with the tic-tac-toe board superimposed on your image. This will help you see how the Rule of Thirds applies to each image you use.*

Perspectives

Photographers create interest by photographing from varied perspectives. Don't always take pictures looking straight on when you can lie on your back looking up, get up high to look down or look parallel to the ground. Photographers also move around subjects to see every side in order to find different aspects of the subject. A plain storefront may have a beautiful mural on its back wall, but you'll never know if you don't circle your subject.

Putting the Image Together

These concepts (centering versus Rule of Thirds; realism versus pop; color versus black and white) work with the technical requirements when photographing. For example, a subject may be isolated from other visual elements in a variety of ways. A photographer might use a telephoto lens to reduce the space around the subject, along with applying wider aperture to minimize the depth of field. In this same scenario, the photographer might find a brightly colored background distracting, so might use a grayscale mode to create a more neutral background.

The most accessible approach to good composition and technique is simplicity. When you photograph a subject, try to approach it with the aim of showcasing the most important person, object or idea. Then, think about what supports or doesn't support that main idea. Distracting elements are objects in the frame that pull our eyes away from the internal, logical flow of the elements that are telling us the story. Light fixtures help us to see, but they appear in too many photographs for no good reason. If the light fixture isn't useful for storytelling, crop it out or move your position. Similarly, look for the edges of doors and window frames, hands, cars, soda pop bottles, trash cans and other objects that people tend to ignore because they are so ubiquitous. Beginning photographers tend to accept these objects as so organic to an environment that they don't think of finding a way to not show them.

Your feet make the greatest cropping tool. By moving around the subject, you can see new things and get rid of others. You can usually remove a distracting element if you zoom in or walk to a new position. Try moving to a new position rather than moving the objects out of the way or erasing them digitally later, as photographers consider these approaches to be unethical.

Simplifying your frame is the easiest way to compose, regardless of whether you center your subject or use the Rule of Thirds, or whether you use color or grayscale mode. This simplicity does not equate to being simplistic. For example, a person moving should be shown with more of the frame ahead of the subject instead of behind it. This lead space allows the viewer to imagine the subject moving through that space. This is simplifying your frame, but a simplistic cropping would crop in on the runner with no lead space at all, isolating the subject from the contextual space.

The following two photos show the difference between a complex composition and a simple composition. (See Figures 6.12 and 6.13.)

The photo of the different flags intentionally confuses the viewer because you don't know where to look, while the photo with the single flag gives direction by following the flag down and to the back.

Figure 6.12
See the companion website, www.focal press.com/cw/filak, for the color figure.

96

Figure 6.13
See the companion website, www.focal press.com/cw/filak, for the color figure.

How to Construct a Picture Series

A picture series also benefits from simplified frames because each photograph offers the viewers a specific aspect of the story. The visual anchor may change photo-to-photo, or the surrounding context or characters may change while the visual anchor remains the same. In either case, the series relies on a thread. For a picture series to become a story, the set of images demands more informational context and a tighter visual thread.

Some publications use online picture galleries to show the public an array images not good enough to make it into the print product. Other publications use the galleries as an opportunity to increase Web traffic. Unfortunately, too many galleries are full of images that fail to interest anyone outside of the friends and family members of the subjects. Because the galleries are a dumping ground for mediocrity, they are not structured in any coherent form.

In contrast to most online picture galleries, photographic series and stories rely on content and ordering. The photographic series is more interpretive than the photo story because there aren't traditional rules of lensing and content. The series of images minimizes context and leaves the audience to interpret the overall meaning. The series often provides little or no text to explain the images, and viewers are encouraged to come to their own interpretation as if listening to a string of interpretive songs.

The photographic story, as photojournalism professor Greg Lewis explains, is based on the seemingly ancient practices of Life magazine. Life editors expected their photographers to return with wide (also known as long) shots for context, medium perspective to bring the viewer into the scene, and close-up shots to show detail. Images should show the subject's faces, interactions with others when applicable, the passage of time or of a sequence when appropriate.

The photo story has evolved since the heyday of Life. Newspapers carried on the photo story, although photojournalists still felt limited by the constraints of space in printed newspapers and magazines. The emergence of online publishing led to initial promises that photo-journalists would get to have more opportunities to do photo stories with as many photos as they desired. The promises quickly dissolved for most photojournalists because of the time required to make a high-quality photo story. Relatively few photojournalists received the opportunities to explore long-form photo stories.

Multimedia Photojournalism

The new visual journalist has to move fluidly between still photography and video recording. One of the biggest challenges is deciding when to shoot stills and when to shoot video, because differences exist between the forms of technology and the approaches to shooting in these media. On the technical side, some newer hybrid cameras – those with still and video options – allow for a still image to be taken in the video mode. Some cameras capture a frame from the video when the user presses the still photography shutter button while the video is being recorded. Other cameras aren't as proficient at recording the still during the video, instead pausing the video for the still to be taken.

Cameras that record 4K-video produce frames of high enough quality to pull and use as a replacement for still shots. As prices drop on 4K, many convergence journalists will choose this format because of its ability to pull stills as needed, without having to worry about quality. The downside to this is the space and time involved in editing. Larger storage devices are needed to hold so many high-resolution frames, and finding the best frame for a still image will require a great investment of time.

Visual journalists who want to be active in both still and video recording need to think about the technology needed to perform hybrid visual journalism. On the side of ease, the best smart phones can record HD video and have a port for microphones. Again, the smaller sensor will produce limitations on image quality. The mirrorless camera systems, in general, take better video than DSLR cameras, and many have ports for microphones. As stated earlier, they are lighter, which is often preferred for multimedia work. Many hybrid cameras are simply still cameras that have movie modes, and their microphones will pick up distracting sounds like a lens zooming.

98

FINAL FOUR

If you take nothing else away from this chapter, here are four things you should remember:

1 The occasional centering of subjects is good, but consistently centering subjects is bad. Move high and low and in a circle to truly understand your subject and create more diversity in your compositions.

2 Look for the strong visual elements such as line weight, movement and repetition of pattern to organize your picture, as well as textures and the ambient color of light to enhance the realism of a photo.

3 Picture galleries should only be as long their ability to maintain interest. Displaying boring photos will make viewers stop looking and possibly leave the site.

4 Photo stories tell their tales through both the variety of the images and the coherence of the message. This form is more engaging than picture galleries but photo stories are more difficult to create.

Further Reading

Hand, M. (2012). *Ubiquitous Photography*. Cambridge, UK: Polity Press.

Kobre, K. (2008). *Photojournalism: The Professionals' Approach*. Waltham, MA: Focal Press.

Kobre, K. (2012). *Videojournalism: Multimedia Storytelling*. Waltham, MA: Focal Press.

Ritchin, F. (2013). *Bending the Frame: Photojournalism, Documentary, and the Citizen*. New York: Aperture Foundation.

References

Ang, T. (2000). *Picture Editing*. Oxford: Focal Press.

Lewis, G. (1996). *Photojournalism: Content and Technique*. Madison, WI: Brown & Benchmark.

Websites

Dpreview Camera and Photography Basics:
http://www.dpreview.com/articles/category/camera-photography-basics

National Press Photographers Association:
https://nppa.org

Nikon FX-Format Sensor:
http://imaging.nikon.com/history/scenes/24/

Nikon Photography Tips and Tutorials:
http://www.nikonusa.com/en/Learn-And-Explore/index.page

Photo.net Photography Forums:
http://photo.net/community/

Information Graphics

Jennifer George-Palilonis

Introduction

Today, information is the most readily available commodity in the world. We have the answers to nearly every question at our fingertips. We carry those answers with us almost everywhere we go on our mobile phones, tablet devices and laptop computers. However, having access to all the answers and understanding them are two different concepts. This is what makes journalism skills more valuable than ever. Collecting, analyzing and deciphering information and then transforming it into stories that are engaging, informative and easy to understand is relevant in nearly every sector of our society. In addition, truly great storytelling is still a valuable commodity and a much-needed skill.

Journalism has changed since the first edition of this book and will continue to change. Newspapers are no longer the kings of the industry and the Internet has given anyone with a connection and a computer the ability to package and disseminate information. Along with heightened access to information comes a greater need for people who can effectively sift through the material they collect, focus on what's important and explain the most complex, impactful stories in ways the average person can easily understand. In this visual age, individuals who can tell stories with images as well as words are extremely important assets in the field of journalism.

Information graphics have been a part of the storytelling landscape since prehistoric people drew the first paintings on cave walls to communicate with one another. Every modern visual editor knows the power of the "show me, don't tell me" approach to explaining the complexities of the world. From graphics that illustrate intricate processes to charts that use simple visual metaphors to represent hundreds of data points in a single frame, well-executed information graphics offer value to both the media and the audiences they serve. Likewise, talented graphics reporters often possess a diverse set of skills, including illustration, writing, research and graphic design. These skills allow those reporters to work with complex data, analyze it carefully and transform it into visual stories that are easy to understand at a glance.

In this chapter, we will explore why information graphics are powerful storytelling tools and the role of the graphics reporter. We will examine several types of information graphics, including maps, charts, diagrams, data visualizations and more. We will also explore what happens to an information graphic as it travels across multiple platforms, from the static print environment to the interactive digital realm. Finally, we will spend some time considering the value of visual reporting skills in our data-rich information age.

The Power of Words and Visuals

During the mid to late 1800s, advances in technology were rapid, prompting what photographer Lloyd Eby called "a profound change in human culture . . . taking us from a literary culture, based primarily on words and printing, to an increasingly image-based, or visual culture." During this time, newspapers, in particular, began to include illustrations, charts and maps in coverage of major news stories. It is important to point out here that while aesthetic appeal is important, information graphics are more than just window dressing. A strong case can be made for visual imagery as a story form in its own right.

Well-executed information graphics help the reader understand and recall information. Studies have shown that while people generally only remember 10 percent of what they hear and 20 percent of what they read, they tend to remember about 80 percent of what they see and do. Cognitive psychologists and researchers who developed and applied Dual Coding Theory (DCT) found that the human mind processes verbal and visual information in separate but interrelated ways. By integrating illustrations with text, or elaborating on illustrations with explanations, both the verbal and visual processing units of the brain are engaged, and memory is likely to be enhanced. In short, information graphics actually stimulate more brainpower than words or visuals alone, leaving a greater impression on working memory.

In this sense, graphics reporters have the best of both worlds when it comes to storytelling. They can examine objects and scenes through rich illustrations that provide visual context and detail that photographs cannot. They can also explore events or phenomena in real time with dynamic animations in ways that videos cannot. They can then combine this engaging imagery with powerful words and rich explanatory audio so that these stories come to life in ways that words alone cannot. However, to effectively achieve these goals, graphics reporters must have a wide array of skills, including the ability to research, write and edit effectively. They must also possess savvy illustration skills and knowledge of a number of complex computer programs.

103

The Role of the Graphics Reporter

Information graphics reporters emerged in print newsrooms in the early 1980s. Many historians and media experts see the newspaper USA Today as the catalyst for the rapid growth of the information graphics industry. The paper adhered to a simple editorial mission: Cater to time-starved readers with tightly edited story packages and an easy-to-read format. This meant shorter stories, innovative application of color and widespread use of information graphics. As the paper began to rapidly expand and other publications followed USA Today's lead, the modern graphics reporter was born.

Just as a good news reporter must write interesting stories, a strong graphics reporter must create visually engaging illustrations. Graphics reporters must possess artistic skills that allow them to create accurate and attractive graphics. However, graphics reporters must first judge their work on the graphic's ability to advance the audience's understanding of a story or event. A good graphic should also offer a clear and accurate presentation of facts. Every artistic decision should consider the needs of the readers, the nature of the story and the clarity of the message. Truly successful graphics reporters are journalists first and artists second.

Graphics reporters perform their roles within a media organization much the same way as other reporters do. They research both the visual and textual elements of their graphics. They consult a variety of sources, including encyclopedias, almanacs, reports and documents for crucial information. They also interview experts to gain additional information and discuss their work with other reporters in the newsroom. Graphics reporters often go on assignments to gather information for their work and they attend news meetings as they contribute to story packages. They must also be accurate, observe ethical journalistic practices and serve as credible sources of information for their audience.

However, the nature of precision differs between a reporter who writes and one who uses charts, graphs and maps to tell stories. The limits of language constrain journalists who only use text to describe scenes. Graphics reporters, on the other hand, can create diagrams that illustrate objects in direct proportion to their real counterparts. They can use texts and visuals to show exactly "what happened," "when it happened" and "in what order it happened." Graphics reporters can also answer key questions like "how much," "how close" or "how did it happen" in a much more concrete fashion than reporters who only use words. Moreover, graphics are often more space-efficient for displaying certain types of information. For example, a chart that outlines the racial composition of the United States is much simpler to read than an enormous paragraph of information. In addition, this form of visual presentation would also make it easier to quickly make numerical comparisons, assess magnitude and fully comprehend the data.

Graphics Typology

Reporters who want to effectively plan and conceptualize their information graphics must understand the types of graphics at their disposal and which ones work the best in which situations. Just like reporters who write, graphics reporters must carefully consider the purpose, news value and message of a graphic before they build it. The reporters must keenly understand the types of graphics they can use, as well as the strengths and weaknesses of each. Most graphics fall into one of the following basic categories:

Simple charts

Even the simplest charts – like pie charts, bar charts and fever charts, to name a few – convey a considerable amount of data in a relatively small amount of space. The nature of the information at hand will dictate which type of graphic the reporter should create. What attracts the eye might not engage the brain, and therefore, effective charts must be clear and precise, accurate and consistent. Here are some simple and yet important rules that will help determine which charts will be most effective in which situations.

Pie charts represent parts of a whole amount broken down into percentages. In this case, a circle is a visual metaphor used to represent the whole. This leads to two critical points. First, the slices of a pie chart must together equal 100 percent, with no exceptions. After all, if the slices of a pie chart amount to 99.9 percent, the readers will wonder what happened to the other 0.1 percent. Second, it is important to indicate the actual numerical value represented by the pie. Without it, the reader has no sense of the relationships between percentages and their actual numbers. For example, 10 percent of 100 is 10, and 10 percent of 100,000 is 10,000. However, the pieces of the pie are the same size in both cases. Graphics reporters must provide the readers with concrete reference points to clearly assess the data in the chart.

Bar charts represent comparisons of whole numbers. The mind can process differences in bar lengths easily, so bars are sized relative to the amounts they represent. If time is a factor, bar charts should be vertical, with dates or times along the x-axis. This is important because, conceptually, time is generally likened to a linear continuum. If time is not a factor, the chart should be horizontal, with the bars ordered from shortest to longest, or longest to shortest. This will make the chart easier to read from left to right. Finally, the graphic should explain the amount each bar represents, so that readers can better understand the underlying numbers.

Fever or line charts plot two related variables to show a trend over time. The y-axis of a fever chart generally plots numbers at equal intervals, with an overall range relative to the data you're presenting. Likewise, equal intervals of time are plotted along the x-axis. Fever charts are most effective when they present a fairly dramatic data set, with many ups and downs.

Figure 7.1

Choropleth maps like the one shown in this Chicago Tribune Olympics package fill each regional boundary (states in this case) with a different shade of the same color. Each shade represents a range of data within a single dataset. Add a few other simple charts, and the result is an engaging visualization.

(SOURCE: "WOMEN IN THE OLYMPICS: THE ROAD TO EQUALITY," LIZ SPANGLER, CHELSEA KARDOKUS AND STEPHANIE MEREDITH, COURTESY OF THE CHICAGO TRIBUNE, COPYRIGHT 2012)

Women in the Olympics: The road to equality

By CHELSEA KARDOKUS and STEPHANIE MEREDITH | Special to the Tribune

Women have competed at the Games since the second Olympics in Paris (1900). Of the 997 Olympians present, 22 were women who participated in just five sports. Fast-forward to 2012 and every participating country has at least one woman on the team, competing in every event, including for the first time boxing.

NUMBER OF WOMEN COMPETING AT THE 2012 GAMES
By country

More than 100 years of progress
NUMBER OF WOMEN COMPETING IN THE SUMMER OLYMPICS *By Games*

2012:
4,833

1900
British tennis player the first woman Olympic champion.

1936
At age 13, diver is the youngest gold medalist in an individual event.

1960
American track athlete breaks three world records in Rome.

2012
Every National Olympic Committee is represented by men and women when Saudi Arabia sends **Sarah Attar** and **Wodjan Shaherkani** to London.

U.S. Olympians by the numbers

For the first time, the United States is sending more women than men to the Olympics. This is partly due to the men's soccer team failing to qualify. Below is a demographic breakdown of the U.S. Olympic athletes competing in London.

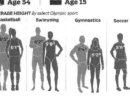

Maps

Maps can present weather forecasts, locate an event or geographically plot statistical information. From the simplest types of maps to the most complex data visualizations, maps help us understand the world. Cartography, or mapmaking, blends geography with a number of other fields, including math, meteorology, statistics, data analysis and more.

While locator maps offer an "x marks the spot" approach, more robust maps show the Earth's formations (geological) or correlate numerical data with geographic locations (statistical). News maps may also explain how and where a specific event unfolded.

Mapmakers can use an infinite number of ways to plot data, but some common statistical maps include choropleth, dot distribution and isoline. Choropleth maps use tones of a single color to represent ranges of data associated with a specific topic and divided by regional boundaries. For example, a choropleth map of the U.S. unemployment rate might color code the data and apply those colors to each of the 50 U.S. states. Dot distribution maps use dots or similar symbols to represent a numerical dataset. For example, a dot distribution map of a large city might illustrate the crime rates in various neighborhoods. After all the dots are placed, the resulting visual pattern allows viewers to understand the distribution of crime across the city at a glance. Finally, isoline maps are most commonly used for reporting weather trends and show continuous lines joining points of the same value. Examples include altitude (contour lines), temperature (isotherms), barometric pressure (isobars), wind speed (isotachs) and wind direction (isogon). Although the terms probably don't sound familiar, we see examples of weather maps every day on the television news, in print and even on our mobile devices.

Diagrams

Diagrams often portray scenes, processes and objects in ways that a picture or words alone cannot. For example, when a crazed tourist attacked the Liberty Bell with a sledgehammer in 2000, a graphics reporter from the Philadelphia Inquirer rushed to the scene, spoke with witnesses and sketched the crime scene. The graphics reporter used this approach to diagram the crime and help readers understand what took place at one of the city's most popular tourist attractions. Likewise, as the nation watched in horror as the Boston Marathon

108

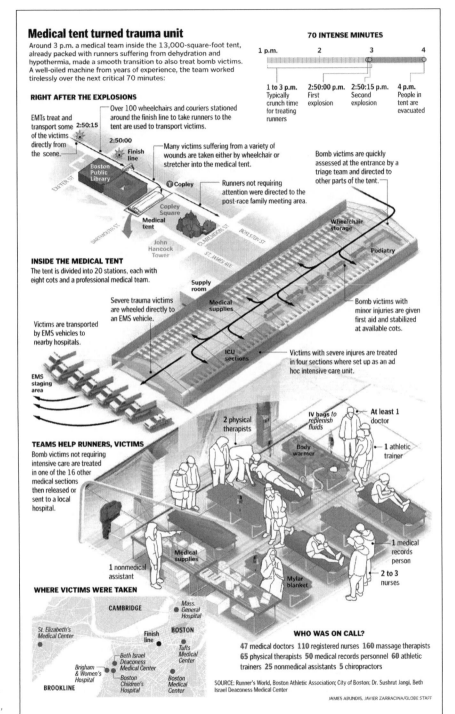

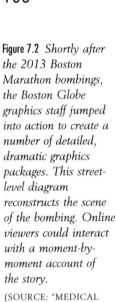

Figure 7.2 *Shortly after the 2013 Boston Marathon bombings, the Boston Globe graphics staff jumped into action to create a number of detailed, dramatic graphics packages. This street-level diagram reconstructs the scene of the bombing. Online viewers could interact with a moment-by-moment account of the story.*

(SOURCE: "MEDICAL TENT TURNED TRAUMA UNIT," JAMES ABUNDIS AND JAVIER ZARRACINA, COURTESY OF THE BOSTON GLOBE, COPYRIGHT 2013)

bombings of 2013 unfolded on live television, the graphic artists and page designers at the Boston Globe used visual storytelling to explain in detail what happened during the bombing, how the victims received medical treatment and the manhunt that followed. From maps that ran in the newspaper less than 24 hours after the bombings, to detailed step-by-step illustrations of how law enforcement officials tracked their suspects, the graphics coverage was dramatic, informative and moving. These examples demonstrate how effective diagrams show how a news event unfolded, the steps of a process or the inner workings of both animate and inanimate objects. Diagrams combine substantial text with detailed illustrations to dissect the important parts of objects or chronicle a chain of events.

Interactivity and Graphics

As graphics migrate to the Web, the potential for animation and interactivity fundamentally changes. Web graphics go a step further than print graphics and provide more immersive user experiences. They can simulate real-world experiences and employ game strategies. They can also use sound and animation to enrich understanding and better reflect reality. Here are several types of interactive graphics and the purposes they serve.

Instructives

Instructive graphics enable the reader to sequentially step through a process, event or phenomena and thus learn "how" something works. Because they are based on sequential information, instructive graphics generally involve two types of user interaction:

1   clicking/tapping through the steps of a process using next/back or numbered buttons; or
2   rolling over or clicking/tapping of a graphic to reveal pop-ups with individual explainers or additional information.

Interactive diagrams and digital maps in which the user is encouraged to explore an in-depth topic or understand a sequential series of events are two great examples of quality instructives.

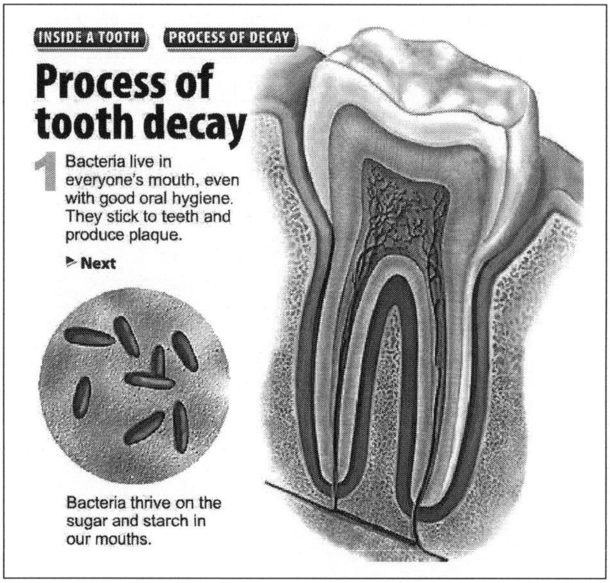

Figure 7.3 *This Sun-Sentinel graphic provides a step-by-step explanation of how tooth decay develops. An instructive interactive, it allows the user to click through each step at his or her own pace.*
(SOURCE: COURTESY OF THE SOUTH FLORIDA SUN-SENTINEL)

Narratives

Instead of written explanations accompanying the illustrations, narrative graphics use an audio voiceover for most of the descriptive content. When a graphic reporter adds engaging visuals and rich animation, these graphics have the potential for highly dynamic presentations that can explain situations or phenomena in real time. Narrative graphics often take the audience where video cannot. For example, an information graphic can explain what happens to the eye during Lasik surgery. A video camera in the operating room would do little more than chronicle the actions of the doctors and nurses. Only an animated narrative graphic can provide a close-up and accurate real-time account of what's going on *in the eye*.

Simulatives

Like instructives, simulatives generally show users how something occurs. However, simulatives go one step further, as they allow the viewer to experience an approximation of some real-word phenomenon. For example, a diagram of an electronic voting machine isn't as

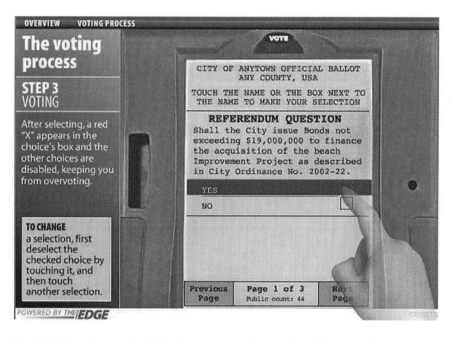

Figure 7.4 *When Broward and Dade counties in Florida adopted new touch-screen voting machines, the Sun-Sentinel created a simulative graphic that allowed users a chance to practice using the machines. Graphics reporters copied the appearance of the machines right down to the typeface that users would see when they engaged with the real thing.*
(SOURCE: COURTESY OF THE SOUTH FLORIDA SUN-SENTINEL)

111

helpful to readers as the experience of using one. A simulative graphic can illustrate the actual look and feel of a voting machine and then allow users to see how it functions. Simulatives are great for any concept that is easily replicated through a computer or other digital device. However, beware of topics where the experience doesn't translate well in the digital environment. For example, "how to plant your garden" might make for a great instructive graphic, but since pushing buttons on a computer keyboard or tapping a touch screen device won't actually dig holes, plant bulbs or water the ground, a simulation isn't the right approach for this topic.

Data visualization

Data journalism is one of hottest topics associated with the digital revolution sweeping the field of journalism today. In "The Data Journalism Handbook", Paul Bradshaw writes,

What makes data journalism different to the rest of journalism? Perhaps it is the new possibilities that open up when you combine the traditional 'nose for news' and ability to tell a compelling story with the sheer scale and range of digital information now available.

(http://datajournalismhandbook.org/1.0/en/introduction_0.html)

Data journalism is a broad term that can be used to define a number of approaches to storytelling. Bradshaw, a professor at Birmingham City University, notes that "those possibilities come at any stage of the journalist's process: using programming to automate the process of gathering and combining information from local government, police, and other civic sources." One great large-scale example is the EveryBlock website, http://chicago.everyblock.com/crime/, which shows criminal activity, from homicides to prostitution, in the city of Chicago. The information comes from CLEARMap, the crime mapping website of the Chicago Police Department, and data is updated each day. Data journalism can also help tell complex stories with engaging, and often interactive, infographics. News organizations like The New York Times, The Washington Post and The Telegraph lead the pack in the use of these tools.

Other organizations have engaged in data visualization as well. For example, Pitch Interactive (www.pitchinteractive.com/beta/index. php), a Berkeley-based data visualization unit, produced a captivating graphic that tracks every drone strike since 2004 carried out by the U.S. against Pakistan. The visualization, titled "Out of Sight, Out of Mind" (http://drones.pitchinteractive.com/) tracks victims of strikes using data from the Bureau for Investigative Journalism, specifically noting children and civilian collateral damage. In an interview with The Huffington Post in March 2012, Wesley Grubbs, who created the visualization, said, "We want to shock people. What we tried to do though with this was not just shock people with the number of casualties, but to shock people with the amount of information that we really don't know." The visualization (which was created in HTML5 and JavaScript) is elegantly presented and effectively daunting. It allows users to examine the data in a number of ways including by attacks and by victims

Mirko Lorenz, a data journalist at Deutsche Welle, sums it up best:

Journalists should see data as an opportunity. They can, for example, reveal how some abstract threat such as unemployment affects people based on their age, gender, education. . . . Using data transforms something abstract into something everyone can understand and relate to.

("The Data Journalism Handbook", http://datajournalismhandbook.org/)

Working Across Platforms

Print and online graphics packages for a single story, as well as partnerships between local newspapers and broadcast news organizations, are relatively common. The New York Times, the South Florida Sun-Sentinel, The Washington Post and others frequently publish graphics in print and on the Web to support their news coverage.

Graphics reporters use a variety of software programs, including illustration programs, animations software, 3D programs and programming languages. These programs allow the reporters to create graphics for print, online and broadcast. The journalists know how to incorporate audio and video into their graphics packages, and they are often called upon to conceptualize a graphic for a single story across two or even three media formats.

Each format provides graphics reporters with specific challenges. Due to the linear nature of print, all of the content must fit into one scene. Without the potential for motion or sound, print graphics reporters must find innovative ways to convey movement and action. Finite space also limits graphics reporters who work to create content for newspapers. However, on the bright side, the reporters can generally produce print graphics quickly.

Broadcast graphics often integrate animation, video and audio, and can provide viewers with a much more realistic portrayal of events. Broadcast news is generally presented in very short, one- to two-minute clips. Thus, a broadcast graphic must convey a point in about 20 to 30 seconds.

Space is virtually unlimited on the Web, and, because it is non-linear in form, graphics reporters can present information in multiple, separate scenes or steps. Add to that the ability to integrate audio, video, text and interactivity, and online graphics can be an incredibly rich, immersive experience for audiences.

So, how does a multimedia graphics package come together? In some cases, reporters from each organization work together to develop the story and gather reference materials. A writer and graphics reporter from the newspaper, a field reporter and videographer from the television station and a producer from the website may work together to conceptualize the entire story package. However, when it comes to the creation of the graphics for all three formats, it's usually more efficient for the same graphics reporter or team of graphics reporters to develop them all. That's because the main illustrations and much of the key information will be shared among all of the graphics.

ONE STORY, THREE GRAPHICS

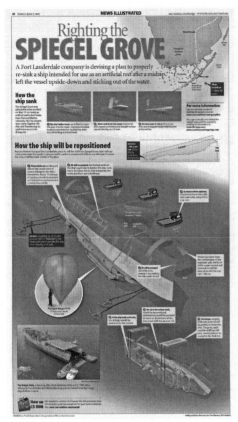

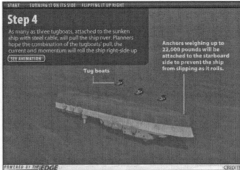

Figure 7.5 *When the Spiegel Grove story broke, a team of graphics reporters at the Sun-Sentinel began working diligently to develop a convergent graphics package that included a component for print, online and broadcast.*
(SOURCE: COURTESY OF THE SOUTH FLORIDA SUN-SENTINEL)

The South Florida Sun-Sentinel in Fort Lauderdale, Florida, was a pioneer in the cross-platform approach to information graphics reporting. In addition to an impressive multimedia gallery of journalistic games, infographic videos, interactives and more (www.sun-sentinel.com/broadband/theedge/), the graphics staff has also produced broadcast graphics aired by its local broadcast news partner, CBS Channel 4 (WFOR).

In 2002, for example, Sun-Sentinel graphics reporters successfully created three graphics packages to cover a single local news story. When Florida officials tried to sink a decommissioned Navy ship, called the "Spiegel Grove", to construct an artificial reef off the coast of South Florida, a mishap left the 5,000-ton vessel upside-down and sticking out of the water for more than a week. Graphics reporters at the Sun-Sentinel covered the story by developing information graphics for print, online and broadcast. Don Wittekind said a team-based approach was adopted for this project.

Graphics were designed to show how a salvage company that was brought in to properly re-sink the vessel was planning to accomplish its goal. The journalism team consisted of five people, each in charge of one of the following responsibilities:

1 Research and reporting and print page production
2 3D modeling of the "Spiegel Grove"
3 3D animation of the 3D "Spiegel Grove" model
4 Web design for online animation
5 Video production and special effects for broadcast

The graphics reporter researched the salvage company, while the 3D artist worked on the model of the ship. As soon as the model was roughed out, the animator took a copy and rendered an image for the print product. Although these were not finished images, they were enough to allow work to continue on three fronts. The Web designer then took the finalized text, along with multiple renders of the ship, and began the online animation. When the final illustration of the ship was ready, the team placed it on the print page and put it into the Web animation. For broadcast, the animation was done, though with an early model of the ship, so reporters only had to update the model and render out the animation. The final step was taking the broadcast illustration into After Effects to add the arrows and special effects. By making sure that everyone was able to work at the same time, all three projects were ready for publication on the same day.

Collaborating with Graphics Reporters

Not everyone will possess the highly specialized skills needed for creating information graphics. Even if your talents lie somewhere else, all storytellers should at least understand the significance and power of information graphics in news coverage. Writers, producers, editors and photographers must recognize when a graphic is necessary as well as how to conceptualize a graphic within a story package. Look for visual cues within a story, and propose a graphic when the answers to the questions "who," "what," "when," "where," "why" or "how" are visual.

Specific numbers, visual descriptions of objects or events and identifiable locations don't always jump out, and a graphic may not always present itself right away. A good journalist will often discover graphics potential in less obvious ways.

VIEW FROM A PRO

DON WITTEKIND

Savvy visual journalists are pioneering new venues for their talents. Swarm Interactive is a design and development firm focused primarily on medical websites and patient education animations. The company's clients have included medical practices, hospital systems and major medical companies. Its patient information system, ViewMedica, is used to help medical professionals explain complex surgical topics to their patients. The ViewMedica patient education system received the Platinum Winner award in the 2013 eHealthcare Leadership Awards for Best Rich Media. Perhaps the most interesting part of the Swarm Interactive story is that it was founded by two former visual editors at the South Florida Sun-Sentinel, Don Wittekind and Scott Horner.

Figure 7.6
Don Wittekind.

Wittekind said that when he took over as graphics director at the Sun-Sentinel, one of his first efforts was to get the rest

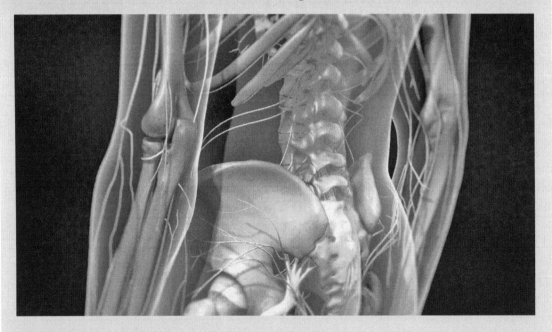

Figure 7.7 *ViewMedica graphic by Swarm Interactive staff.*
(SOURCE: COURTESY OF SWARM INTERACTIVE)

of the staff trained in how to produce multimedia graphics. At the time, the newspaper produced a weekly full-page science graphic called News Illustrated, so that was an obvious place to start for developing a multimedia strategy.

"On one of my rounds through the department, I noticed that Lynn Occhiuzzo was working on a News Illustrated about a new spinal fusion technique," Wittekind said. "Lynn has had multiple spine surgeries, so this is an area of interest for her. I mentioned that a surgery was a great topic for an animated graphic, and [Horner] and I worked with her to produce an interactive to go along with the newspaper graphic. This is 1998, so we were working in Macromedia Director. Flash did not exist."

The day the print and online graphics were published, Occhiuzzo told Wittekind she was taking a framed version of the print page to her doctor. She had promised him one in exchange for being her source for the graphic. While at his office, she also showed him the animation produced for the newspaper website. He liked the print graphic, but when he saw the animation, he told her, "I have to have that!" When Occhiuzzo got back to the office, she called Wittekind.

"I thought she was resigning, because she was so nervous," he said. "When we sat down, she said, 'I just told a bunch of doctors we could build websites and make animations for them. Can we?'"

At first, Wittekind laughed and told her he didn't know but would ask the editor, Earl Maucker.

"I asked if he minded if a few of us worked on some medical websites and animations for an orthopedic practice," Wittekind said. "He said that was not in competition with a newspaper and was fine as long as we did it on our own time – standard freelance policy. So we took the job and ended up building three sites and nine animations for that first group of doctors."

At the time, the graphics reporters didn't even own copies of the programs they would use for these projects, and they were expensive. So they downloaded 30-day trial versions of Director and Dreamweaver and used them to build the sites and animations. By the time the trials were up, they had our first payment from the doctors and were able to buy the software.

"We never took a single loan, even from ourselves," Wittekind said.

They didn't need to. They had storytelling skills, and on those skills alone, Swarm Interactive was born.

Swarm remained a part-time enterprise from 1998 until 2006. At that point, the company's monthly income from licensing rose to a level that could support a full-time employee. So Wittekind moved to Chapel Hill to teach at University of North Carolina and build the company. He hired Daniel Niblock away from the Sun-Sentinel to be Swarm's first employee and lead multimedia developer.

From there, things took off quickly. Within a few months Wittekind convinced Occhiuzzo to leave the Miami Herald and move to Chapel Hill to become Swarm's chief operations officer. The company later hired another former co-worker from the Sun-Sentinel.

"After just a couple of years, I had half of my former Sun-Sentinel graphics staff working at Swarm," he said.

Wittekind said the hardest transition was learning to run a full-time business, which isn't taught in most journalism schools.

"Managing a staff was no problem," he said. "I did that for 10 years at the Sun-Sentinel, so I had a comfort level there. But suddenly I had to find and implement a company insurance plan. And you have to offer a 401K plan. So many things that business people take for granted were brand new and very difficult for me. A full-time business is very different from being a freelancer. Don't underestimate the differences."

Through it all, Wittekind said his belief in his team's ability to tell stories never wavered.

"Every industry has stories to tell and difficult topics to explain, so our skills are in high demand in many areas other than journalism," he said. "Unfortunately, there are a *lot* of former journalists out looking for work, so it is important to set yourself apart."

118

Once you determine that a story needs a graphic, you should begin conceptualizing what form the graphic should take, as well how the graphic might change across two or three platforms. If it's a print graphic, be aware of how much space is available, and understand how to present all of the information in one area. When you develop the graphic for the Web, consider the ways in which interactivity can enhance a viewer's comprehension. You want to determine what kind of presentation – narrative, simulative, instructive – will be most helpful in the audience's efforts to understand the information at hand and how will animation and interactivity affect a user's navigation of the content.

Depending on the nature of the story and the timeframe of the deadline, the creation of graphics for any format could take anywhere from a few hours to a few weeks. Ultimately, information graphics are an extremely powerful storytelling method for all kinds of journalists. They often take readers where cameras or reporters cannot. They simplify complicated information and give it a visual context, capitalizing on the fact that most people tend to understand better when text and images are combined.

Ultimately, the storytelling potential of information graphics reporters is limitless, and it's up to you to capitalize.

THINKING ABOUT ADDING GRAPHICS

Here are some key questions to ask as you ponder the value of adding a graphic:

- Is the explanation in a story getting bogged down and difficult to follow?
- Is there information that can be conveyed conceptually to put a thought or idea into a more visual perspective?
- Who are the key players and why?
- What are the key dates?
- How did we get here?
- Where do we go from here?
- What's at issue, and what does it mean for the audience?

119

FINAL FOUR

If you take nothing else away from this chapter, here are four things you should remember:

1 Well-executed information graphics are powerful storytelling tools because they seamlessly, richly and dynamically blend words and visuals in ways that stimulate the brain.

2 Visual reporters are just like journalists who write. They dig deep into all kinds of sources, from visual references to expert sources. They scrutinize, analyze and make big decisions about how important stories are produced and presented.

3 All journalists should be able to spot graphics potential in a story. Use graphics to help explain complex information, organize information in a more digestible way and elucidate the most important parts of a story.

4 Every industry has stories to tell and difficult topics to explain. Visual reporting skills are valued in nearly every sector of society in our digital age. Don't limit yourself to working in traditional news environments.

Audio and Video Journalism

Erika Engstrom and Gary Larson

Introduction

Good storytelling remains dependent on good writing and understanding how the value-added features of sound and pictures combine with the words to convey information. This said, the use of audio and video in journalism allows the reporter (storyteller) to add the "show" to the "tell." When done correctly, mixing text, audio components and visual elements helps audiences learn about events and remember information that impacts their lives.

In this chapter, we will cover the basic principles required to make the added value of sounds and images to a broadcast news or Web story worth readers' and viewers' time. We will also cover how to write for this form of journalism in a way that will help your audience consume the information you present to them.

Writing for the Ear

Relaying information to your audience comes down to teaching your listeners and viewers what you believe is important. The successful conveyance of an event or issue requires you to communicate the facts as if you were actually talking to your audience. Writing for the ear means writing the way you talk – as if you are starting off the story with, "Hey, did you hear about . . . ?" The essence of writing for the ear includes both knowing how to write clearly and concisely, as well as ensuring a smooth delivery for the person actually reading the script.

For reporters and anchors, who may or may not do their own writing, conversational style reflects a convergence between the written word and the spoken word. Writing in short sentences in simple subject–verb–object sequence characterizes the "easy to understand the first time" quality of broadcast newswriting. (For more on stylistic aspects of this form of writing, see Chapter 2.)

Show and Tell: How It Helps the Audience

The addition of audio and video becomes a way to increase the potential for learning and understanding on the part of the audience, with the narration enhanced by an additional mode of conveying information. As mentioned in Chapter 7, this is known as dual coding, which means that the listener or viewer receives information via two "codes" or channels. We typically see dual coding in the form of video being narrated by a reporter or anchor. The spoken words accompany the images on screen and we both hear and see the information.

Onscreen graphics, whether as an over-the-shoulder graphic or a full-screen graphic during a television news story, also provide dual coding. The use of visuals that relate to the audio portion of a news story increases the potential for recalling that information later – we associate the words spoken with an image because they have been received via more than one code.

Word and Picture Overlap

Researchers of television news consistently note that people tend to have greater understanding, recall and interest when television news stories are presented with interesting visuals. However, because people watching the news split their attention between the sound and the images, it is important to build a certain degree of redundancy into a news story. Also called semantic overlap, this means that the video should match the audio narration and vice versa – if a full-screen graphic of text is shown onscreen, the narration the anchor provides should match the words onscreen.

Too much overlap between the verbal and visual, however, can be just as detrimental as too little. If you have audio and video that present identical information, you can bore or offend your audience members. Good journalists strive to strike a balance when it comes to this issue.

Most information gain occurs when the video portion of a television news story complements the audio narration. If the words don't match the pictures, audience members must decipher the onscreen visuals at the cost of paying attention to the audio narration. Research has found that, when this happens, people tend to create more negative thoughts about the story and its presentation. Mismatching video and audio has been found to impair learning. Whoever writes a news story should also know what video footage will accompany it. Writers must work closely with the production team members who will visually translate the news story script into what will appear onscreen.

Similarly, when an audio-only soundbite is used in a radio or podcast news story, the story copy should explain who is talking during the soundbite. The time constraints of radio and television news, however, require the writer to be economic with words and pictures so the maximum amount of information is conveyed in a minimum amount of time.

123

Audio

Radio is the original form of broadcast journalism. The addition of the recorded or live words of a news source is the audio version of the direct quote in print news – and serves much the same function as quotes in newspaper and online stories. Radio (or audio) journalism relies on three story forms based on the use of audio:

1   the reader
2   the wrap-around
3   the package.

In radio, newscasts typically make use of all formats.

The reader

In a reader, the announcer reads the story in a straightforward manner on the air. This is the easiest way to get the news to the audience. Readers are the shortest story form time-wise and typically run between 15 to 20 seconds.

The wrap-around

The wrap-around uses reporter copy to introduce a soundbite and then uses additional copy to augment what the source said. The anchor reads the story, introduces the recorded actuality then continues with the rest of the story. Wrap-arounds can include up to two soundbites before the story becomes cumbersome and confusing.

A good analogy of the wrap-around is a sandwich – the script before and after the actuality could be considered two pieces of bread and the actuality is the filling. Wrap-arounds are read live during a newscast, with either the anchor or the producers playing the actuality at the proper point of the story. Wrap-around stories can run between 40 and 45 seconds.

HOW TO PRESENT THE SOUNDBITE

When introducing an actuality/soundbite, the anchor should

1 identify the person speaking with his or her name and title
2 provide a hint as to what the listener will hear.

Redundancy in the case of introducing a soundbite prepares the listener for the actuality itself without using the same words the source is using. You need to avoid using the exact words that are heard in the soundbite as the introduction for the soundbite. Also, don't be lazy in your writing – to introduce a soundbite with "So and so had this to say" is just as bad as parroting the source in the introduction. It takes no training to write, " . . . had this to say."

Here are some examples. The colon at the end of the intro sentence means a soundbite is to follow. After each introduction, read the recorded audio transcript to hear how each intro sounds:

Recorded audio from Mayor Roberta Roberts chosen as a soundbite
It's really a matter of whether or not we value our children's education, so this sales tax increase shows that improving our education system has finally become the topmost consideration in our community.

Bad: The "parrot" introduction
MAYOR ROBERTA ROBERTS SAYS IT'S REALLY A MATTER OF WHETHER OR NOT WE VALUE OUR CHILDREN'S EDUCATION:

Just as bad or even worse: The "lazy" introduction
MAYOR ROBERTA ROBERTS HAD THIS TO SAY:

Better: The paraphrase set-up
MAYOR ROBERTA ROBERTS SAYS THAT VOTERS HAVE SHOWN THAT THEY'RE WILLING TO PAY AN EXTRA FEW CENTS AT THE CASH REGISTER FOR BETTER PUBLIC SCHOOLS:

The soundbite itself usually lasts no more than 15 seconds. The actuality you choose should be something that the interviewee says that you cannot paraphrase without losing its impact. Just like a tasty sandwich filling, choose a sentence or two from an interviewee that adds flavor to your story. Actualities should contain information that you can't say better yourself – it should be "colorful" in terms of the language used and provide interest as well as information.

When choosing soundbites from interviews, the audio quality itself needs to be good. The source's voice should be clear and free of invasive background noise. Too much natural sound drowning out the speaker's words will make the actuality unusable. If the background sound is more prominent than the source's words, the listener will focus on the noise, which negates the purpose of getting a source to speak to you.

Before leaving a scene or the interview, a brief playback is a good idea so that, if necessary, you can rerecord the interview. This is also a good idea for recorded phone interviews, so you don't have to call the source back or try to find another source when you're on a deadline. It is better to discard a bad piece of audio rather than using it and detracting from the story.

NATURAL SOUND

The inclusion of natural sound can provide an aural context for the listener and an immediacy to the story itself. In a story about an outdoor music festival, for instance, faint music would add value and depth to the piece. However, if the music itself is louder than the speaker's voice, then the soundbites you collect will be worthless.

A short excerpt of natural sound can serve as actuality, as long as it is preceded by an introduction so the listener knows what the sound is and as long as the natural sound is discernible. In feature or human-interest stories, natural sound adds context and variety. The sound of hooves clopping on cobblestones in a feature story about a blacksmith who crafts horseshoes, for instance, gives the story an added dimension.

Use natural sound in audio-only stories with care. Effective use of natural sound requires clear, recognizable sounds and noises that precede a brief description in the script. For example, a reporter could include a few seconds of parade sounds before saying something like, "Today's Saint Patrick's Day Parade transformed downtown into a multicultural celebration." The script serves to confirm what the listeners suspect: They have just heard the sounds of a parade. Conversely, the same sentence could be used to introduce the natural sound, which would prepare the listeners for what they will hear next. The same principles of intros and outros used in audio news apply to video stories as well, as we discuss later in the section on video.

The package

The long form of the audio news story is the package. The term "package" implies it is self-contained and ready to give, just like a wrapped gift. Reporters usually produce their own packages in radio news, but editors may prepare some packages. Packages typically include soundbites from two sources, but two soundbites from the same source can work as well. The reporter is also responsible for writing the introduction to the package, which the news anchor will read on the air.

An introduction similar to the introduction that precedes an actuality in a wrap-around will precede a package. This form of storytelling usually runs from 60 seconds to 90 seconds. The introduction to the package itself should run no longer than 15 seconds.

Video

Television news stories are written in the same broadcast style as radio news, but the added element of video requires more information to be included on a page of script. TV news scripts thus are written in a double-column format, with the video information, including shot instructions and visual graphics, on the left side and the audio portion on the right side.

Just as any radio journalist should be able to read a script that someone else wrote, TV news scripts are written so that they can be aired without having to ask the writer any questions. In other words, the writers should have composed the script so that it can be handed off to others and easily understood.

TV NEWS SCRIPT EXAMPLE

TV NEW VO SCRIPT EXAMPLE

ALADDIN VO 9/21 6 PM WRITER: JONES	(STEPHANIE)
ANCHOR ON CAM E: ALADDIN	A LAS VEGAS LANDMARK IS CLOSING ITS DOORS TODAY.
START ENG/VO :00-:20	THE ALADDIN HOTEL-CASINO ENDS ITS 34 YEARS ON THE STRIP AS IT
CG: ALADDIN HOTEL-CASINO	MAKES WAY FOR A NEW RESORT. CLOSE TO 15-HUNDRED EMPLOYEES ARE BEING LET GO. THE HOTEL'S 17- STORY TOWER IS TO BE IMPLODED NEXT WEEK … IT'LL BE THE FIFTH IMPLOSION HERE IN THE PAST FOUR YEARS. A NEW ALADDIN IS IN THE WORKS, WITH PLANS CALLING FOR 26- HUNDRED ROOMS AND A NEW MUSIC-
END ENG	THEMED HOTEL NEXT DOOR.

Figure 8.1 *A sample of a television script, which details both the words the reporter will speak and the elements that will appear on the screen during this story.*

In this example of a television news script for a VO, the left side indicates what will appear on screen and the right side indicates what the anchor reads. ANCHOR ON CAM means the story starts with the anchor on camera. E: ALADDIN means there is an effect titled "Aladdin." This tells the director to superimpose a graphic illustrating the story over the shoulder of the anchor. START ENG/VO means to roll the video (ENG stands for electronic news gathering, the term for "videotape"). The anchor reads the story as the video plays on-screen. CG: indicates what text will appear superimposed over the video as it plays. END ENG means the story is completed. The half-underlines on the right side of the script let the anchor know when the videotape will start and when the story and video ends. The video portion of this story is assigned 20 seconds of newscast time.

Assignment editors traditionally assign videographers and reporters to stories based on the news plan for the day. The editors listen to the police and fire department scanners for breaking news and read news releases as well to determine what merits news coverage.

Reporters and videographers typically work together to cover news events. The reporter takes notes at the scene, conducts interviews and writes the story. The videographer decides what to shoot, sets up the equipment for interviews and records the reporter's stand-up or live shot. Both members of the team understand what makes for good writing and good video and they often assist each other throughout the process.

Video News Story Formats

Television newscasts rely on four basic forms of video storytelling, from simplest and shortest to most complex and longest:

1 the story read by the anchor on camera live during a newscast, known as an on-cam reader
2 the voice-over (VO)
3 the voice-over sound-on-tape (VOSOT)
4 the package.

Newscast producers decide which story format to use for each story they include. These story formats serve as the television versions of radio news stories, only now visuals accompany the verbal portion.

The on-cam reader

The on-cam reader story might have just the anchor speaking, or it could have an over-the-shoulder graphic onscreen while the anchor reads the story. The onscreen graphic, created by the production team, typically consists of some kind of still photo or computer-generated picture and text that relates to the story itself. Again, the idea is to infuse the graphic with some redundancy with the news story copy so that it complements what the anchor says. Readers typically last 15 to 20 seconds.

The VO

The VO (voice-over) is basically narrated video. The anchor reads the news script over the video. The VO usually begins with the anchor onscreen for a sentence. At the beginning of the second sentence of the story, the screen cuts to video footage that has been edited to the script, with just a few extra seconds of video as padding in case the anchor reads the story more quickly than expected. An onscreen graphic or CG is superimposed over the lower part of the screen to indicate the geographic location of the story (such as city and state, or city and country). VOs typically run from 15 to 20 seconds, but more complicated VOs may run as long as 30 seconds.

The VOSOT

The VOSOT (voice-over sound-on-tape) serves as the video version of the wrap-around. The anchor is first on camera, and then the screen will cut to edited video that plays while the anchor reads the story. The video is broken up with a soundbite, with more video to follow. The VOSOT begins with the anchor onscreen reading the first sentence, and the VO starting usually at the start of the second sentence. The timing of the VO portion of the story is crucial, because the video editor relies on the timing indicated in the script to edit in the soundbite. The video editor then adds the remaining footage for the rest of the story which consists of the anchor-narrated VO. VOSOTs typically run from 30 to 45 seconds.

129

A soundbite source is identified during the soundbite video with an onscreen graphic usually consisting of two lines of text. The graphic normally includes the source's name and title, which is either an occupation or a short note explaining why that person matters to the story. For example, it would be irrelevant to identify a witness to an accident with an occupation (for example, "accountant"). Instead, audience members would rather know how that person mattered to the story (for example, "accident witness"). As the writer of the story, you would be responsible for providing the production team with all the names and titles of the people involved in the soundbites.

The package

The package is really a recorded VOSOT that a reporter narrates and a videographer assembles. The anchor introduces the television package during the newscast itself. Even though the package is a self-contained, recorded story, it does require a scripted introduction. A good package intro uses enough detail to engage the viewers as it sets up the story to come. Similar to the introduction to a soundbite, a package intro should give a hint about the story itself, rather than simply telling the viewer that the reporter "has the story."

Sometime during the package itself, the reporter makes an appearance in a "stand-up." Stand-ups locate reporters at a scene, and allow them to comment on what is going on or what happened at that locale. The point of stand-ups is to place reporters in the field. These can be useful to fill in information for which there is no video or provide solid transitions between two disparate parts of a story. From more of a marketing standpoint, the stand-up can provide some interactivity between the reporter and the audience and provide an opportunity to attach the station ID to the story at hand.

In the stand-up, reporters become involved in the storytelling without actually becoming part of the story. However, sometimes reporters serve as participants for human-interest stories that require demonstrations – for example, a reporter might participate in a sporting event or celebratory festival to show viewers what it's like to be there as well as to provide additional visual interest for a story.

130

THE VIDEO ESSAY

The video essay (or audio visual montage) contains video and natural sound edited in such a way as to tell a story without relying on voice-over narration. The images, natural sound and soundbites carry the storyline of an event or theme. Music may serve as the soundtrack as well.

The video essay is usually reserved for stories with high emotional content or for stories where the visuals are too complex or emotional for narration. The essay relies on the idea that a picture is worth a thousand words. At one end of the emotional spectrum, a video essay might reinforce the violence and horror of a disaster, such as the attacks in New York City on September 11, 2001. At the other end, video of a hot air balloon festival can use the colorful balloons and surrounding landscape to tell a happy and peaceful tale.

With the videographer serving as the producer, reporter and editor of the story, the video essay format allows for a greater degree of creativity and expression.

Video in a Converged Environment

The concept of converged media is important because it seeks to draw an audience from demographics that do not consume traditional news formats. While baby boomers watch newscasts from beginning to end, read daily newspapers and perhaps even listen to National Public Radio in their cars on the way to work, millenials generally rely on digital devices to consume news in small bites. This should not be read as saying either the boomers or the millenials are "worse" than each other. They each simply employ different news consumption habits. Convergence efforts allow journalists to reach these groups in a way that best reflects how the group members consume news.

Converged media production could not have happened without two things: The development of digital video and the development of the bandwidth necessary to carry that video on the Web. We are now at the point where content and technology come together to provide the possibility of a rich, multimedia experience for viewers.

One of the bigger issues pertaining to video and the Web is the concept of "shovelware." This term refers to the transferring of content from traditional to digital platforms without a sense of the differences between the two. In print, this can mean copying and pasting a story from a newspaper to the Web. In broadcast, it usually means cutting story packages from a nightly newscast or stripping off the video from a TV broadcast and running the audio as a streaming sound or podcast file.

In some cases, these simple transfers make sense. The audiences between the platforms may differ, and thus the Web audience won't be seeing a rehash of what it already saw on the TV news. The approach is also easy, because it uses material that is already available and thus doubles the reach of the material with almost no effort. In other cases, the shovelware approach is just about being lazy and not adjusting your thinking when it comes to a convergent environment. Some video stories could be longer or shorter for Web audiences, depending on the content of the story and the interest level of the viewers. On-cam readers could be repackaged into a series of simple text briefs, as having the anchor read them for the Web offers almost no value.

The approaches to video journalism here all have value on both traditional and digital platforms. The trick to doing this kind of work well on the Web is to understand which forms of broadcast journalism

131

VIDEO TERMINOLOGY

Video journalists have a terminology unique to their profession. Most of that terminology describes the various camera movements and shots used to create a strong video narrative. Below is a series of terms that video journalists use to describe camera movements and types of shots.

Pan, zoom and tilt

These moves occur without moving the supporting tripod or pedestal. A panning shot moves the lens in a horizontal direction, while a tilt moves the lens in a vertical direction. A zoom draws a subject closer via the manipulation of the lens. Not all lenses are zoom or "variable focal length" lenses, but they have become the standard in videography.

Push and pull

These movements are also made with the zoom lens, but where a zoom is done while the camera is in stand-by mode to set up a shot, both pushes and pulls are slow zooms either toward the subject (push) or away from the subject (pull), done while the camera is in record mode.

Dolly and truck

These moves involve not only the camera and lens, but also the tripod or pedestal to which the camera and lens are attached. A dolly moves the camera closer to or farther away from the subject, while a truck moves the camera horizontally to the subject. These moves generally require a lot of space and, while used heavily in film production, are not used as much in journalistic videography.

Establishing, long, medium and close-up shots

These types of shots represent the way film and video is typically shot for playback on a large screen or a television monitor. The establishing shot is typically a shot that sets the environment around a story. It could be a long shot of an apartment complex where firefighters battle a blaze or the inside room of a business where a newsworthy event took place. A long shot is taken from a distance, thus allowing the videographer to capture a wider swath of a scene. A medium shot presents video that is akin to what viewers would normally see with the naked eye. A close-up shot lets viewers see details that may not be apparent in a wider shot.

Cover and cutaway shots

These shots are taken specifically for the editing (or "post-production") process. Cover video is generally close-ups of hands performing some task. It should be a shot of something germane to the story being told. Cutaway video is more generic and is often B-roll (or secondary) video of the general scene. B-roll is used to visualize a news script, and is used to "fill in the gaps" between primary video, such as soundbites.

translate best to the Web for each story and then approach your content accordingly.

When *Not* to Use Video

The assumption for many people in the world of converged journalism is that video should be used for every story, which is not true. Video (or any other production element) should be used only when it can help tell a story in an effective manner.

Most viewers of converged journalism sites do not want to watch a video of a city council meeting. Unless a reporter can find some compelling reason to use video, a text-based story would likely be a better approach to the topic. If the journalist decides to use video, however, video quality is certainly something to consider.

Video Quality

A story can be exceptionally compelling, but if the video quality is bad, you will have an ugly story. If you pay attention during the acquisition of video, you will have access to good video elements during the editing process that will make a story stand out.

Sound issues

Nothing ruins a video faster than bad audio. Journalists should be using equipment that features professional, grounded audio inputs (commonly called XLR). Whether microphones are wireless or wired, having a good mic and professional inputs will solve many problems. Journalists should plug a set of headphones into the camera to make sure they are getting good audio. Do not rely on the camera to adjust its own audio through "auto gain" circuits or other automated camera features. Manual control of audio is not difficult and is part of the videographer's art.

Lighting problems

Backlighting happens when a journalist positions a subject in front of a window or other bright, light-colored surface. The iris within the lens of the camera determines how much light will fall onto the light-sensitive chips within the camera. Positioning the subject like this will make it almost impossible to get good video.

133

Close the iris down to limit the light and your subject soon become a silhouette with no defining features at all. Open the iris up to get features on your subject, and the light coming from the background will cause the whole video frame to lose definition (commonly called "blown-out video"). The solution is to reposition your subject away from the light.

Visual interest

Video shot during interviews that will later be used for soundbites should contain some visual interest as well. Placing a news source within the context of his or her work or expertise, rather than at a desk, will provide visual interest and further enhance the source's value within the story. Similarly, the background visuals for reporter stand-ups for packages should place that reporter at the scene or in a context related to the story.

Take advantage of the environment and position your interviewees where lighting is optimal and the background adds something to the visuals. It could be as simple as moving an interview to another part of a room or even down the hall where some semblance of visual variety is happening. Always be aware of where you are, no matter if you are the reporter or the videographer. Creativity on the part of both team members, and appreciation for each other's strengths and ideas, will help to produce good quality video and stories.

These two reporter stand-ups were both shot at the same Renaissance Faire. The reporter stand-up in Figure 8.2 is framed well, but a bit boring. In comparison, the reporter in the stand-up in Figure 8.3 took advantage of the costumes available from an event vendor, creating a more creative and lighthearted image, inviting the viewer into the narrative of the story.

This reporter stand-up shows creativity, but it does not show well on small screens. Keep monitor size in mind when framing a shot to meet the criteria for good video on the Web.

The composition of this video serves as an example of good framing. While this shot is acceptable, the background could use a bit more visual interest (see Figure 8.4).

Video on the Web

Where and how your audience members access your video will determine if the video does a good job of conveying information to

Figure 8.2 *A standard version of a stand-up at a Renaissance Faire. This is simple, but a bit boring. However, it gets the job done.*

Figure 8.3 *An innovative approach to a stand-up at a Renaissance Faire. This reporter demonstrated a deeper level of engagement with the topic and was willing to try something different.*

them. A small screen, such as a phone or tablet, will accentuate shaky video, so use a tripod, monopod or some other device to hold your camera steady. A small screen will make long and establishing shots almost worthless unless the subject of the shot is scenic, so avoid these shots and concentrate on medium and close-up shots for your story. Use close-up and extreme close-up shots to heighten emotion, and medium shots for the bulk of your story. Finally, framing your shots can have a great impact, so remember to frame your video appropriately. (See Chapter 6 for a discussion of framing rules.)

Moving away from technology and into content, webcasting generally means individual short stories rather than full newscasts. In cases where the website is an offshoot of a television station, individual stories can be cut from the latest broadcast for inclusion on the website. The real downside of webcasting for many journalists is the

Figure 8.4 *Long shots like this one tend to play poorly on small video screens like phones. Consider your media platform before selecting video shots like this.*

Figure 8.5 *Medium shots of interview subjects play well on tablets and phones. Consider moving subjects to areas where they are easy to film and that add value to the overall interview.*

loss of the more traditional news cycle. With the advent of first 24-hour cable news and then the Web, journalists have less time to get their stories produced, let alone actually thinking deeper about the implications of their stories for the communities they serve.

Shovelware, as noted above, refers to content posted on a station's website that comes directly from television newscasts. It's easy to post packages or newscast segments without any editing, and to upload story scripts from a reporter's computer. Because they are essentially self-contained entities, the package makes the optimal news story format for the Web.

The package easily translates to an audio-video story on a news station's website, as it can be uploaded, basically, "as is." The uploading of text in the form of a written package intro, along with hyperlinks within that text, essentially completes the process for posting a television news package online. For stories that were initially aired as live shots during a newscast, however, the in-studio anchor intro-duction is usually included in the posted video story. Other formats, such as the on-cam reader, the VO or VOSOT, don't lend themselves that well to an online version. These can easily be rewritten as print-only stories, with hyperlinks to their corresponding video, as long as that video is not too short.

VIEW FROM A PRO

JOE W. MORRISON JR.

Joe W. Morrison Jr. is an Emmy Award-winning journalist with nearly 30 years of broadcast news experience as a videographer, editor and producer. Morrison now owns a full-service video production company in central Florida, and produces a wide range of video projects for non-profit entities, legal firms, small businesses and families.

Figure 8.6
Joe W. Morrison Jr.

In his career as a videographer and editor, Morrison has shot and edited video for nearly every kind of story imaginable. He says that no matter what the subject matter – whether hard news or human interest features – good video is compelling.

"Good video makes you want to see more," Morrison said. "It stimulates the senses, entertains you and educates you. Good video takes you to another place and makes you glad you have eyes and ears." Lousy or poor video, on the other hand, does not connect viewers to the words being spoken in the telling of a story and the pictures being shown onscreen, which is the same conclusion that researchers have known for years regarding the overlap required for enhanced recall and understanding.

Whether it is a camera or an audio recorder, familiarity with the tools used for gathering audio and video is of utmost importance, he said. Morrison always has a battle plan before stepping out of the newsroom, but keeps his eyes and ears open for the unexpected.

"I always plan out ahead of time what I want to accomplish during a shoot," Morrison said. "You can do this, and yet still leave room (and time) for creative, spontaneous and unexpected things that might come up during the shoot, and they almost always do come up, thank goodness."

The interplay of audio and video can never be understated, Morrison said, noting that even professionals can make ugly mistakes in this area.

"I've seen many shoots ruined because the videographer was too lazy to mic the subject or didn't monitor audio while recording it," he said. "I don't want bad audio to distract me and keep me from enjoying a story."

According to Morrison, future journalists must be able to work both in front of and behind the camera. Knowing what makes for good newswriting and good video is essential, especially in today's television news environment, Morrison added.

"Journalism today is an industry in a state of transition," he said. "Since newsroom staffers may be asked to do numerous jobs, it helps to have a wide variety of skills. There is never a substitute for good storytelling abilities."

FINAL FOUR

If you take nothing else away from this chapter, here are four things you should remember:

1 It's about storytelling. The basics of good storytelling serve as a foundation that prepares the videographer and the reporter to communicate information effectively to the audience. Beyond video that excites or grabs the attention of the viewer, use audio and video to tell the story.

2 It's about quality – technical and artistic. Good video has the potential to make an emotional impact on viewers. Skilled videographers apply their training as artists to spot interesting visual elements that relay emotion in some way as part of the larger story they are telling.

3 It's about knowing your equipment, through and through. Good audio and video require familiarity with the equipment. Audio and video are equally important in broadcast newsgathering. Extra noise, distracting sound and poor fidelity will kill a radio story. Poor audio, in turn, will kill even the best video.

4 It's about caring. Take pride in your craft and appreciate the effort it takes in bringing the news of the world to the people listening and watching your work. In the hectic world of broadcast and Web journalism you need to get it fast, but not at the expense of getting it right. The good journalist is always concerned about producing high-quality work.

Further Reading

Bock, M. A. (2011). "You really, truly have to 'be there': Video journalism as a social and material construction." *Journalism and Mass Communication Quarterly, 88*, 705–718.

Conway, M., & Patterson, J. (2008). "Today's top story? An agenda-setting and recall experiment involving television and Internet news." *Southwestern Mass Communication Journal, 24*(1), 31–48.

Fox, J., Lang, A., Chung, Y., Lee, S., Schwartz, N., & Potter, D. (2004). "Picture this: Effects of graphics on the processing of television news." *Journal of Broadcasting and Electronic Media, 48*, 646–674.

Gotfredson, D., & Engstrom, E. (1996). "Video essay: Teaching and learning with alternative news presentations." *Journalism and Mass Communication Educator, 51*(2), 55–62.

Graber, D. (1990). "Seeing is remembering: How visuals contribute to learning from television news." *Journal of Communication, 40*, 134–155.

Schultz, B. (2005). *Broadcast news producing.* Thousand Oaks, CA: Sage.

Zhou, S. (2005). "Effects of arousing visuals and redundancy on cognitive assessment of television news." *Journal of Broadcasting and Electronic Media, 49*, 23–42.

Data-driven Journalism

Bob Britten

Introduction

When you hear "data," you might think numbers. You might also think, "I got into journalism to avoid that kind of thing!" Believe it or not, though, you're more familiar with managing data than you might think. If you're cleaning up your room after a long time, there's a lot to go through. First, you decide what to keep (possessions) and what to discard (garbage). If the "keep" pile is large, you can sort it into more manageable groups: Clothes, books, office supplies and electronics. These may have subcategories: Clothes are dirty or clean; books are yours or borrowed, and so on.

With your piles sorted out, you make conclusions. The books need to go back on the shelf, to a friend or to the library. The clothes need to be washed or put away. Office supplies could go into the drawer you always check for something to write with. Further, you might make larger realizations. Perhaps you find you have too many red T-shirts, that you use a lot of blue pens or that you rarely read the books you borrow from the library. These revelations, in turn, might translate into a change in your actions.

Congratulations, you've just managed some data! Taking a bunch of things, sorting them and using them to answer specific questions is what data journalism and information architecture are about.

This chapter is largely written for newcomers, but it will contain jumping-off points throughout for those with a little more expertise.

We'll talk about data journalism in four stages. First, we will explore what data is and why it matters in journalism. Next, we will discuss how to identify, isolate and access the specific data you need when faced with a world of data points. Then, we will examine how to make that data coherent and meaningful. Finally, we will discuss some basic data visualization techniques that can help you tell a compelling story.

Thinking with Data

Data is a collection of facts. It might be numerical, but it might also consist of words like names or political parties. You might find it organized into a detailed and well-formatted spreadsheet, or it might be encased in paragraphs of narrative text, waiting to be extracted. If you're dealing with a series of values that can be listed, counted or compared, you're dealing with data.

Types of data

At the broadest level, data can be qualitative or quantitative. Qualitative data describes the qualities of something: Its name, flavor, color and so on. Quantitative data is numerical, such as the weight of a child or the number of robberies in a month. You can also see this distinction in the different levels of how we categorize data.

There are other types of data within these two, as our room-cleaning example showed. Categorical (or nominal) data, for example, is a typically qualitative type that consists of mutually exclusive (non-overlapping) categories – in your room, an item can either be in the "possession" category or the "garbage" category, not both. Another is ordinal data, which describes rank – an example would be the range of grades (from "poor" to "gem mint") of those baseball cards you found under your bed.

Numerical data can be either discrete or continuous. Discrete data consists of whole numbers with gaps – the number of shirts you find, for example, is discrete (you won't find 3.7 shirts, unless you have a poorly trained dog). In continuous data, all values in a range are possible – the pens you find might be completely full of ink (1), completely empty (0), half full (0.5), a third full (0.333) or any other value.

Data Journalism

Data journalism exists in asking questions of data. The questions you ask determine both which data you seek and what you do with the data. One cold January morning, you might think, "This winter seems colder than usual." To determine if this supposition is true, you must identify the data you need. You can identify the variables (measured items that can have different values) associated with this topic: "Winter cold" and "the past few years."

Right now, these variables are abstract and can mean a variety of things. "A few years," for example, can mean the past three, five or ten years. You need to operationalize your variables by defining them in a specific, measureable way. Since you made your original observation in January, you might operationalize "winter cold" as the average January temperature. If you decide that you only want to study the years in which you have lived in your current state, you could operationalize your term in that fashion.

Once you know what data you want, you must find it. Let's start at the top. A reliable source might be the National Oceanic and Atmospheric Administration (NOAA), which in turn is host to the National Climatic Data Center (www.ncdc.noaa.gov). This organization's site "provides free access to NCDC's archive of historical weather and climate data." After specifying your location, date range and desired data (average temperature), you can download a spreadsheet with this information.

You now have data in hand, but raw data can't answer questions on its own. In a data set displaying only the past 10 average January temperatures, it's fairly easy to see which is lowest, but many data sets are much larger. Using a spreadsheet, you could apply a formula to determine which temperature is the lowest, or one that calculates the mean of these temperatures. If this year is the lowest, you have just found some support for your original assumption.

The above example is just a sample. You can find many ways of asking and answering this kind of question. Interrogating the data meaningfully, creatively and thoroughly is necessary for good storytelling. First, however, you have to *get* that data.

Getting Data

Data is everywhere today. We can see it all around us – in the social media we use, the purchases we make and so forth – but that doesn't mean we know how to get at the data. In fact, so much data exists that deciding on some tiny slice of it to use can feel quite daunting. As with any journalistic story, it is important to determine which story you want to tell.

For example, let's say you want to write a story on arrests made in your town. Your first stop is going to be the police department. Once you decide if you are interested in city police, campus police or state police arrests, the next question is what information each organization has available. Some police stations now save all records to a publicly accessible database, although others still rely largely on ink and paper. As a reporter, you may hope for the most convenient format, but you should plan for the worst-case scenario.

Working with Paper Data

Regardless of the wealth of information seemingly available at our fingertips, there remain many times when you just need to get on your feet, get out of the door and do some in-the-flesh reporting.

In our example, let us say you decided that you want to report on campus crime and then identified the questions your story should answer – "Have thefts increased?" "Are public drunkenness reports changing?" After identifying your data needs, you head to the campus security headquarters and request all theft complaints and public drunkenness reports from the past five years.

The desk officer informs you that these records are available only as handwritten documents sorted (more or less) by date. The good news is, they can readily point you toward the years you want. The bad news is, you need to sift through all of them on your own. In addition, the records may not leave the office, and the police won't make copies for you.

Most police departments today use digital tools to some extent in their record keeping, so there's a good chance records exist in PDF or even spreadsheet form. The point of this scenario is that it could happen, either in part or in whole, and that means you will need to put forth some serious transcription efforts. Your tools in such a case are, at minimum:

- A laptop computer or tablet (because you need to be mobile)
- A spreadsheet or database application (such as Excel) with which you are familiar
- A notepad and pencil for recording observations, possible trends, and new questions that arise while you're immersed in the data

Using paper and pencil may seem old-fashioned, but one strength of that approach is that it allows you to take notes in a separate place while entering hard data on your laptop. Another reason is that the end product of your work will likely be visual – perhaps a table or chart – so you want to be able to sketch out visualization ideas as they occur to you. Having a place to take loose, free-form notes complements the structured format of your spreadsheet.

Digital Data

The previous section addressed how to deal with analog data, but it's increasingly likely that the data you want will be digital. In acquiring such data, the first steps are the same, but where and how you look will be different. In the digital world, you can go looking for data in the format that you prefer. This section addresses three areas of digital data acquisition: Running searches, writing scrapers and filing FOIA requests.

Searching

Even if you know how to use a search engine, you probably haven't had much experience using one to find specific data. You can limit and filter your search to seek certain objects, to exclude others or to examine only certain web pages. The more precise you are, the more precise your results can be.

Make your search as specific as possible, identifying particular phrases, domains and file types for the search engine to seek. Much of the process will be trial-and-error. If one search does not turn up useful results, you can modify or remove restrictions, one at a time, until you find a search that works.

Scraping

A scraper is a computer-based tool used to examine some part of the Internet for specified data. That part could be an application such as Twitter or a specific part of the Web, such as a government agency's

USING SEARCH OPERATORS

Search operators are commands used to narrow or broaden the range of a search. The operators identified below are common but not universal (most will work in Google), so test them out on your search engine to be sure (also note that operators using a colon (:) cannot have a space after the colon).

Including and excluding results:

- Exact matches. When you type more than a single word into a search engine, it will typically seek those words as a phrase but also as individual words. To search only an *exact* phrase, put it in quotation marks ("flying fish of the Pacific Ocean").
  - Alternative 1. Use the "AND" operator to return only hits with all specified terms – "ham AND eggs".
  - Alternative 2. The "+" operator signifies certain mandatory terms among several – "green +chinese +pottery" would require Chinese pottery results but be lenient about the color if few involved green.
  - Alternative 3. The "allintext" operator does essentially the same thing, but only looks within the body text (not the title, link, or URL) of a site – searching "recipe allintext: eggs turmeric cinnamon" would only return recipes including all three of those ingredients.

- Excluding words or phrases. Sometimes you're searching for a term or something with a meaning that isn't the most common use of that term. "How to clean a bass," for example, would primarily yield results for the fish, but that's not helpful if you meant the musical instrument. The "-" (or "NOT") operator excludes unwanted results: "how to clean a bass -fish" provides information that's more in line with what you seek.

- Either-or searches. Use the "OR" operator to find any results that have at least one of the specified terms ("franks OR beans").

- Synonyms. Use the "~" operator to include results that have similar meanings to the specified term ("~ugly").

- Incomplete words or phrases. If you know some but not all of the search term you need, use the "wild card" (*) operator.

- When seeking a particular phrase, it is most effective to pair this operator with quotation marks ("Ask not what your * can do for *").
- This operator can be used to seek a particular file type ("*.pdf"), but using "filetype:" is preferable (see below). The wild card operator is useful if you want all cases of a file type that include a particular word (e.g., "*crime*.pdf").

• Compound queries. Mix AND, OR and NOT (Boolean) searches by using parentheses ("theft AND (property OR vehicle)").

Dates, numbers and file types:

• Numerical ranges. Use the ".." operator between the top and bottom ends of your range. Searching "25..35 mpg" would yield results for cars within that range. Use only one value to limit only the bottom (30..) or top (..50) of your search's range.
• Specific dates. Use "daterange:" followed by a six-digit numeral in year-date (no hyphen) format. The search "Boston daterange:201303" would return only results from March (month 03) 2013.
• Searching within a specific site or domain. Use this if you want data from a specific domain – "site:.gov" – or site – "site:snopes.com". You can also add search terms to this as usual – "tenure site:.edu".
• Searching for a particular file type. Use this to seek data formats that fit your needs. If you're planning to do the work in an Excel spreadsheet, which uses the ".xls" extension, you can use "filetype:" to seek only results of that type – "crime rates filetype:.xls".

147

statistics page. Building something like this might sound intimidating, but if you can conduct a search or use a spreadsheet, you can write a simple scraper. Unlike a search, which is a one-time entry, a data scraper is a dedicated tool.

In many cases, if you can read it, you can scrape it. Web scraping, for example, is focused specifically on information from websites. It is based on recognizing elements of markup languages such as HTML and extracting the information contained within specified tags.

> ### OUTWIT HUB
>
> A more complex but still accessible option is Outwit Hub (outwit.com), a tool that scrapes websites and breaks them down into their structural components to get at the information you seek. According to its creators, Outwit Hub lets users "harvest data elements, documents or media from virtually any public (and legal) source of content." It exists as both an add-on to the Firefox browser and as a standalone app and has free and paid versions.

Coders develop complex, powerful scrapers using languages such as Ruby and Python. Learning such skills and languages is a demanding but rewarding path. However, developing these language skills is not the only way to create scrapers. Sites such as ScraperWiki provide simple tools for scraping Twitter for data to return as a spreadsheet.

148

How to write a simple scraper

Google provides spreadsheet capabilities via its Drive application. One of its handiest tools is a function called ImportHTML that allows you to import tables and lists from websites. Some other spreadsheet applications have their own means of importing Web content, but ImportHTML will serve here as a quick illustration of scraping.

Once you find a data table online you want to use, first check to be sure you can use it (for more on this see the next section on the legal implications of scraping) and that it's not already available for download. If it checks out, you can start scraping. We'll use publicly available government data (see the discussion of public vs. proprietary data below): An unemployment rate table from the Bureau of Labor Statistics.

You need the site's URL (including "http://"), the data's format ("table") and its number (2). The data's "number" will be based on how many similar elements exist on the page. For example, if you want to scrape a table's data and three other tables are above it on the page, you would use "4" in the index spot listed below. With that information, create a new spreadsheet in Drive. Enter the following function in the first cell of the spreadsheet:

=importHTML("URL", "format", index)

Each of your parameters should be included in the appropriate place. Don't forget to include quotation marks around the first two, which are string (rather than numerical) values – this will be discussed further in this chapter's section on spreadsheets. The Bureau of Labor Statistics data we are using is monthly unemployment rates from 2004 to 2014 and is the third table on the page, so the formula would read:

=importHTML ("http://data.bls.gov/timeseries/LNS14000000", "table", 3)

If it doesn't work, check first for syntax (those quotation marks, commas and parentheses really do matter), and try adjusting the index of your table (if 1 didn't work, try 2). Once successful, you can work with the spreadsheet in Drive or download it (File > Download) to your computer.

The legal implications of scraping

Just because something is on the Web, it does not mean you are free to use it for your own purposes. Some sites address scraping in their terms of use, although these are not always enforceable. On the one hand, U.S. legal precedent holds that facts are not copyrightable because they "do not owe their origin to an act of authorship" (Feist Publications Inc. vs. Rural Telephone Service Co. (1991)). On the other hand is the reality of proprietary data, an organization's internally generated data that allows it to compete. Using a for-profit organization's proprietary data without consent takes away from that organization's ability to profit from its own work and, in most cases, doing so oversteps both legal and ethical bounds.

For journalists, scraped data has two acceptable origins: Official government/public sources and proprietary data that has been provided with the consent of its originator. The data you use must be either publicly available or you must have permission to use it. Anything else – for legal and ethical reasons – is off limits.

FOIA requests

One approach to gathering data that straddles the old and new is the Freedom of Information Act (FOIA) request. Established in 1966, FOIA establishes any American's right "to obtain access to federal agency records, except to the extent that such records (or portions of them) are protected from public disclosure by one of nine exemptions or by one of three special law enforcement record exclusions" (foia. gov). This right can be made for any non-exempt record, and it is enforceable in court.

According to foia.gov, an FOIA request has three requirements: "[It] must be in writing, reasonably describe the information you seek, and comply with specific agency requirements." That last point can vary widely, although the site says most agencies today accept electronic requests. A list of details for federal agencies is available at www.foia. gov/report-makerequest.html.

FOIA does not require agencies do any new research, answer specific questions or create the records you want them to have. They must only provide the records they actually have. You need to have a clear and specific idea of the kinds of data you're seeking in advance of making the request.

Working with Data

After you make your request for data or engage in some legal scraping processes, you still have some work to do before the data set is usable. Your information is likely in a raw (or primary) form. This means that the data currently exist only in a massive block without context or formatting. Raw data is problematic on its own because it doesn't provide the necessary information for comparison, and meaningful comparison is at the heart of data journalism.

In any data-based narrative, the central question must be "Compared to what?" A massive database is not useful without some meaningful comparison that allows the reader to understand what seven of X or a million of Y means. To that end, this section will cover the topics of normalization and formatting.

Normalization

If you wanted to track murders in the United States, for example, you likely would find more murders in Texas, California and New York than in North Dakota, Vermont and Wyoming. It does not, however, mean that you are more likely to be murdered in the first group of states than in the second.

Reporting the raw numbers is not valid because you haven't converted the data to a form that can be meaningfully compared. By normalizing the murders against a value such as state population – dividing the first by the second – we can find the murder rate per state resident. A state with more people may have a higher raw number of murders but the same (or even lower) rate as a much less populous state.

Other comparative factors come into play here as well. Illinois, for example, includes the city of Chicago and its surrounding regions, which the FBI reported had 500 murders in 2013. It may not be that murders are as common in the rest of Illinois as they are in Chicago.

CHICAGO CRIME

This is also a great example of why we need to interrogate data closely. In 2013, the FBI released its annual crime statistics for the previous year. The dataset placed the city of Chicago at the top, with 500 murders. Fox News Channel reported on this as "FBI: Chicago officially America's murder capital," with the number of murders almost 70 greater than the previous year (New York, it noted, saw almost 100 fewer).

Chicago reporter Mason Johnson took Fox News to task for this, explaining that the Chicago area's murder rate was 7.1 per 100,000 residents, lower than the Detroit, Philadelphia, and Baltimore areas but also Alabama's areas of Montgomery, Mobile, and Birmingham. The use of "area," he explained, includes a much larger region than the city proper (Chicago's city homicide rate alone is 18.4), but this is the region by which the FBI classifies all such metropolitan areas. He also added that even the FBI had "cautioned against using these statistics for ranking purposes."

The Fox News story *did* acknowledge the idea of the murder rate, but only to say that Flint, Michigan, had a higher rate than either New York City or Chicago. Sometimes the headline isn't the real story.

Source: Johnson, M. "Chicago not actually 'murder capital' of, well, anything." http://chicago.cbslocal.com/2013/09/26/chicago-not-actually-murder-capital-of-well-anything/

Formatting

In addition to normalizing the data, you need to format it. If you receive data in a less convenient format, such as in hard-copy form, you will need to do considerably more work to make it manageable. In almost all cases, cleaning and formatting will be necessary.

Clean entries

This is the first and last thing to check with any collection of data. This item is in many ways the simplest, yet it's also the easiest to disregard. A misspelled item, for example, is an item that won't be counted, and that's an error. A good first step to avoiding this is running the spelling check application, but this can't be the only step you take. Any report will be laden with jargon, terms specific to the field but less familiar to readers. You should scan your data visually to look for errors. Ideally, a second party will also have a look, especially if you entered the data yourself.

We will use our campus crime example to illustrate this. Many crime reports involve issuing a citation, so you might expect to see this word often. But, every so often, your fingers (or those of the reporting officer) might slip, turning "citation" into "citaiton." Perhaps one officer records as "Theft (Property)" what another records as "Property Theft." Without correcting idiosyncrasies like these, your data will be incomplete. It might seem less significant when dealing with a spreadsheet containing thousands of entries, yet every absence is an inaccuracy that can lessen the credibility of your reporting.

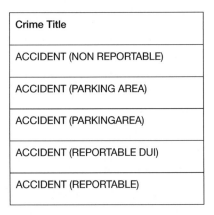

Crime Title
ACCIDENT (NON REPORTABLE)
ACCIDENT (PARKING AREA)
ACCIDENT (PARKINGAREA)
ACCIDENT (REPORTABLE DUI)
ACCIDENT (REPORTABLE)

Figure 9.1 *Although all of these things might be the same to you, they are all different to data-analysis programs. Make sure you standardize the items in your data set before you analyze it.*

Clear categorization

In our campus crime report, we would need the date, time and location of crimes. We want to know what kinds of crimes were committed. It might be important to know the "who" as well here, but in many cases that information is not available.

The above examples are fairly universal: A thing happened at a time and place and involved specific people. In some data sets, categories can be more specific to the particular group. As an example, let's add a column to our example: "Disposition." In police jargon, this refers to the status of the case. A case may be listed as "open," "closed," "cleared," or "arrest." "Open" and "arrest" may seem fairly straightforward, but you might not know the difference between "closed" and "cleared." Before you decide to combine these categories, you should determine how meaningful this distinction is to your research.

Consistent formatting

This goes hand-in-hand with cleaning, but is a little more involved. Even if you obtain data from a highly professional and reputable organization, you can't assume it is free of error or contradiction. For example, if the department switched from reporting on a 12-hour (a.m. and p.m.) system to a 24-hour one, you will have problems comparing all the data values within the set.

In our campus crime example, consider the "Location" category. One of your reporting interests is thefts at the Student Recreation Center. However, you notice that this is logged differently depending on the reporting officer – some list it as "Student Recreation Center," some as "Student Rec Center" and some as "SRC." This is a significant concern because it puts you at risk of incomplete reporting, so you need to fix it before you analyze your data set.

153

Using Spreadsheets

Unless you work with a small amount of data, you will need an application to help you keep track of it all. Applications like spreadsheets and databases store your data and let you sort and calculate it.

For the purposes of illustration, this section will use two widely used spreadsheet applications: Microsoft Excel and Google Drive. Excel is part of the Microsoft Office package, a common fixture in many newsrooms and university computer systems. Drive is part of the Google suite of applications, and you can use it for free if you have a Google ID.

First, know how many variables you will need. Each category will have a column, so it's important those categories be designated as clearly as possible (a header row is strongly recommended). Each row

Date Occurred	Time Occurred	Case Number	Crime Title
8/25/2011	12:04:00	11-0011264	THEFT (BUILDING)
8/31/2011	17:03:00	11-0011687	ACCIDENT (PARKING AREA)

Figure 9.2 *This is a simple breakdown of crime data based on a few key variables.*

is a single entry, such as the date, time, type and disposition of an individual crime report (see Figure 9.2).

When all the entries have been entered, you can seek the answers to your questions. Simple sorting is a good first step. Depending on the focus of your questions (time, location, etc.), try sorting the data by those criteria:

- In Excel: Data > Sort, then select the column to sort by (e.g., "Date") and ascending (low-to-high) or descending (high-to-low) order.
- In Drive: Select the column you want to sort by (e.g., Column B), then select Data > Sort Sheet by Column B.

Patterns could emerge from your data set after this sort. Perhaps Thursdays appear more frequently than other days, or perhaps a particular dorm building seems like a hotbed of activity. At this point, you are only doing a visual check, but doing so first gives you an idea of where you might want to focus.

Bringing in formulas

Once you have an idea of where you want to go, you have to start counting these records. One way to do this is with a pen and paper, counting each relevant entry individually. This is slow, inflexible and subject to human error. A far better solution is the use of formulas. A formula is a statement in a spreadsheet that begins with an "=" sign, telling the application what you're up to.

There are two parts to a formula – the function and its parameters:

- Function: The component that immediately follows the "=" sign and tells the spreadsheet what to do. Examples are SUM, AVERAGE, MAX and SUMIF.

- Parameters: The conditions that must be met and what happens if they are (or are not). They are contained within the parentheses following the function. Parameters may involve:

  - A single cell (e.g., "A1" or "F17")
  - A range of cells ("A1:A100" or "H7:H12")

The SUM function, for example, adds all the cells in a given range of cells. If you wanted to add the values from cell A1 to cell A10, you would select the cell where you want this sum to appear and enter =SUM(A1:A10). In this example, the colon (:) indicates the entire range of cells between the two cells you've selected. More complex formulas involve two or more parameters and can even call other functions within their parameters.

USEFUL FORMULAS

These formulas are a good set to begin with. Every formula must begin with an "=" sign to work. Another common problem is forgetting punctuation such as commas, quotation marks or closing parentheses. If something is going wrong, check the punctuation first.

- COUNT(range): Counts the number of values in a range (e.g., "A1:A10").
- SUM(range): Adds up the values in a range.
- AVERAGE(range): Averages the values in a range.
- MAX(range): Identifies the largest value in a range. There is also MIN, which finds the smallest value.
- DAY(cell): Returns a numeral 1–31 for the day of the month in a cell that contains a date such as 8/25/2011. There are similar functions for WEEKDAY (1–7), MONTH (1–12), and YEAR, as well as for HOUR (0–23), MINUTE(00–59), and even SECOND (00–60).
- Conditional ("IF") functions are more complex but also more powerful because they allow greater sorting and comparison of data.
- IF(logical test, value if true, value if false): Checks another cell's value against some criteria. If it passes (true), one value is reported; if it fails, the other is. For example: IF(A1>0, "YES", "NO") would report YES if the value in cell A1 is greater than zero and NO if it is not.
- COUNTIF(range, criteria): Counts all the values that pass a test criterion. Examples might be "TRUE" or "Democrat" or ">10".
- SUMIF(range, criteria): Sums all values that pass a test criterion. Tests are similar to those for COUNTIF, but this function can only be used on cells with numerical (not string) values.

AN EXAMPLE WITH COUNTIF

If you wanted to find the number of Thefts in your crime data quickly, you would use the COUNTIF function. This function counts all the cells in a selected range that match a value you determine. It has two parameters – range and a test criterion. Be sure your data is clean, clear and consistent because the function will only recognize cells with the *exact* value you enter.

For the range, we will assume that the times of crime reports are in column D, and there are 100 entries in total, so the range will be D2:D101 (it doesn't begin with D1 because there is a header row). The test criterion will be "Theft" – the quotation marks are necessary because this is a string (non-numerical) value. The final function will look like this:

=COUNTIF(D2:D101,"Theft")

To count all crime types, you can apply the COUNTIF formula to each crime type you'll be visualizing, using their different names. We'll do this in the visualization section later in the chapter.

COUNTIF is useful for tallying single variables, but even more useful is the ability to count up the values that match more than one variable test. For this, use the COUNTIFS function (don't forget that "S"). This function uses a range-criteria pair like COUNTIF, but it counts up values that meet multiple tests rather than just one. If you wanted to only count up thefts from October, you would test for two criteria: Crime type ("Theft") and Month ("October"). If Months were in column H, the final function would be:

=COUNTIFS(D2:D101,"Theft",H2:H101,"October")

Further, if you had multiple years of data but only wanted October thefts from 2012 (with years in column J), you would add an additional range-criterion pair, resulting in:

=COUNTIFS(D D2:D101,"Theft",H2:H101,"October", J2:J101,"2012")

Once that data has been sorted and counted, it needs to be presented in an understandable format. Doing this requires visualization, which will be discussed in the next section.

Visualizing Data

Understanding nonlinearity is key to much of data journalism. "Nonlinear" is a term which here means "not in a straight line." This stands in contrast to a traditional text-focused narrative that is (intended to be) read from start to finish. It is difficult to start a text narrative at a paragraph or sentence of your choosing, but, with a data narrative, that is often exactly what the reader is expected to do. The complexity with which this is made possible, however, ranges from simple analog formats like the table to highly structured digital approaches. Before data can be visualized, however, it must be structured in a format meaningful to readers.

The LATCH approach

One of the most common approaches to information architecture is LATCH, an acronym information architect Richard Saul Wurman coined that stands for Location, Alphabet, Time, Category and Hierarchy. Each describes a different way of classifying information. A good choice is one that adds a layer to the data through the comparison it provides. A poor choice does not add value, and may even confuse readers' ability to read meaningful comparisons.

- Location: Where are the individual values in your data situated? For example, if you're working with U.S. Census data, much of it will be linked to states and municipalities, allowing comparisons of their populations, demographics and so on. Crime data might be tied to specific street addresses that can be shown on a map. An effective location-based structure is one that tells the reader something more about the sets of locations the data describes. It is based on a story whose central question is "where?"
- Alphabetical: This approach is often the default, but in most cases it is the least informative way to structure data. Unless your interest is in designing a list, such as a phone book, this approach is arbitrary and adds little to the data. Think about it: Although a number of words in your database may start with "A," does this mean they have anything in common?
- Time: Just like place, information can be pegged to a particular time. If the story you want to tell deals with many points in a particular period, time may be the structuring element you want to consider. A time-based story is focused on questions of "when?" or "how long?"
- Category: This element examines how data points group together around a single consistent factor. This approach to data can involve existing types, such as gender, race or religion, or new types that the observer creates based on the data.

- Hierarchy: This refers to the magnitude of the data. Hierarchical data may be ranked most to least, largest to smallest and so on. The ordinal data type discussed above would be a clear fit for a hierarchical structure.

Applying the LATCH structure to your narrative allows you to focus on an area. Will your readers be most interested in finding their state? Use Location. Would your readers want the most recent numbers? Apply Time ordering. Do you think they just want to see the highest or lowest scores? Use Hierarchy as your guiding principle. Each one creates a different narrative. With this in mind, we can now consider the format in which the data will be presented.

VIEW FROM A PRO

GRANT SMITH

Grant Smith's job is all about finding patterns. As a data reporter with The Commercial Appeal in Memphis, Tennessee, his job is to collect and corral the data into meaningful stories, asking what are the trends, omissions and revelations in a data set.

"I get to have my hands in lots of different cookie jars," he said. "I think a data reporter is essentially a beat reporter, but instead of covering city hall, I cover and interview data. Of course I talk to real people too, but my beat is data and all the trappings that come along with that."

Smith said his job requires the ability to see patterns in the world, not just in data. His job relies on the scientific method, which starts with formulating a question, not being handed a spreadsheet. A database of crimes committed in an area, for example, initially presents more questions than answers: Are these numbers higher than expected? Lower? How should the numbers be compared? What should be reported? It's also

Figure 9.3
Grant Smith.

important, he said, not to get too attached to your initial ideas: A data journalist must be able to form hypotheses and predictions about the world and be willing to disprove them.

A data journalist's job is not identical from day to day, but, in a typical cycle, Smith might have to update data (e.g., salaries, homicides or crime trends) on the Web, work on public records requests and work on his own stories. In addition, he said, "probably half of my time is spent working with others," so his job often involves talking to reporters about their projects to see if he might be able to contribute reporting or interactive data elements. Somewhere in there he also tries to commit time to longer-term projects.

One such major project is The Commercial Appeal's homicide tracker (www.commercial appeal.com/data/homicide). Part of their website's Data Center, this ongoing project uses Google Fusion Tables to present an up-to-date picture of homicides in the Memphis region. When Smith adds a homicide, the tracker updates the page's data breakdown about homicides, their resolutions, their locations and the means by which they were committed.

The process, he said, is one of ongoing development: "First we had to acknowledge that we had an unfilled need; check out what other folks have done; figure out what data fields need to be collected; explore technology that would work; and then actually build it, an hour here, a couple hours there. . . . In addition to being a great resource for the community, it's also a dataset we never had before."

There's no specific list of tools a data journalist must know, but learning readily available ones such as Excel and Google Fusion Tables is a good start. For the next steps, Smith recommended R-Statistics, Javascript and MySQL, as well as Web development tools. More important to the job, though, is the ability to learn new skills quickly. "Keep abreast of new tools. If a job is best done with Python, learn enough Python to do that job."

Visualization formats

Only at the end of the process does a data journalist decide on a format for the data. The needs of the story should dictate the visual form you use. The realm of information graphics is more fully covered in Chapter 7, but here we'll touch on three common forms for visualizing a complete data narrative.

- Lists: A list visualizes data based on a single variable in a vertical format. It is quick and easy, but it is also the most simple of displays. For example, you might list the states' populations alphabetically or hierarchically (most to least). The phone book is, in essence, a list – functional but not revealing of much depth.
- Tables: A table is another simple form of nonlinear narrative, but you have far more potential in that simplicity. A table is a matrix

of rows and columns, each representing a variable, and each individual cell is a particular interaction. Those values can be quantitative numerals (numbers of votes for different candidates x individual districts) or qualitative strings (different issues x candidates' stances on them).

• Charts: Charts deal with quantitative data. They are more complex to create, but provide a more visual and focused narrative. If your story emphasizes the "how much?" question, a chart may be appropriate. Most charts are based on area (e.g., pie charts) or an X-Y axis (bar or line charts). An area chart can show a proportion or parts of a whole; bar and line charts can show differences across time or location. Going back to the types of data discussed at the start of the chapter, a bar chart deals in discrete numbers over time or place while a line chart shows continuous data, single numbers that change over time (such as temperature).

We can consider visualization using our campus crime example. Let's say you wanted to examine the frequency of police reports

Months	Crime Totals
January	320
February	312
March	302
April	286
May	149
June	90
July	121
August	260
September	337
October	261
November	237
December	201

Figure 9.4 *A frequency table that outlines crime data in a month-by-month approach.*

throughout the year. (See Figure 9.4.) The type of visualization you use depends on the story you want to tell. The simplest visualization would be a list of reports by month, which is a good place for your spreadsheet's =COUNTIF function.

This format, organized by Time, doesn't allow much distinction, so we can't tell the type or severity of the reports, but it does illustrate how tied up the police are each month.

Moving a level up, we might want to visualize specific types of reports throughout the year. (See Figure 9.5.) This requires two variables: Types of Crime (Category) and Time of Year (Time). A table provides greater specificity of values but lacks visual immediacy; a chart quickly and clearly shows trends but does not provide precise data to the reader.

We'll use a table first. This example counts the eight most common or notable types of report and leaves the remainder in a category called "Other." It is organized vertically by month (Time) and horizontally by report frequency (Hierarchy). We can clearly see the most frequent reports are for liquor law violations and the rarest are for arson.

Month	Liquor	Drug	Theft	Traffic	Battery	Harass	Robbery	Arson	Other
January	62	76	19	11	2	6	0	0	144
February	53	78	34	12	4	3	1	0	127
March	54	31	18	17	2	5	0	0	175
April	59	34	29	6	5	1	0	0	152
May	7	7	15	12	1	0	1	0	106
June	1	0	7	9	4	2	0	0	67
July	5	1	12	18	1	0	0	0	84
August	58	45	16	28	2	2	1	0	108
September	65	47	23	15	5	1	0	0	181
October	56	42	12	17	7	4	0	1	122
November	12	48	17	10	8	0	0	0	142
December	24	34	16	16	0	1	1	1	108
TOTALS	456	443	218	171	41	25	4	2	1516

Figure 9.5 *A month-by-month breakdown of various crimes in a spreadsheet format.*

This format reveals precise numbers, but it is difficult to get a picture of how those numbers relate, so we'll try a chart. (See Figure 9.6.)

Our data is for 2011–2012, so in this chart the months have been rearranged to follow the August–May academic year. In this format, there are visible distinctions between reports in months when students are present all month (September, October, January, February), when they have breaks (August, November, December, March, April), and when few are on campus (May, June, July). Liquor and drug violations are high during peak student times, low in others. We also see, however, that thefts keep close to a far more consistent frequency – there is still a summer dip, but not nearly so large.

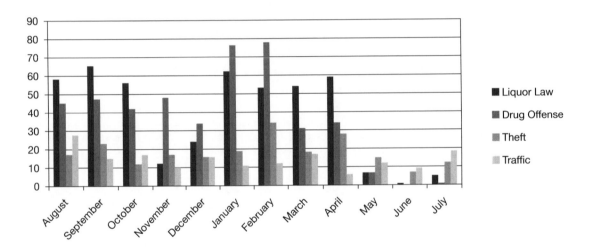

Figure 9.6 *Putting the data from the table above in chart form makes it easier for readers to conceptualize when most crime occurred and what type of crime it was.*

FINAL FOUR

If you take nothing else away from this chapter, here are four things you should remember:

1 Data on its own is not magical. Asking the right questions of it determines what it can tell you. Make sure your questions are based on identifiable variables that can be searched out and examined.

2 Hone your skills of data acquisition – *all* of them. Scraping is just one route to data. So are search engines and FOIA requests. Don't pigeonhole yourself, and you'll be more difficult to shut out.

3 Comparison is key. A given number or statement only becomes compelling in the context of others. The story lies in how it is bigger, smaller, better, worse or otherwise different.

4 No one visualization fits all stories. A sharp-looking chart has its place, but so does a simple list. Know the right tool for the narrative that needs to be told.

Social Media

Sara Steffes Hansen

Introduction

Social media generates quite a buzz in journalism these days. The excitement centers on the ways in which it allows journalists to produce work and interact with society. In addition, social media gives readers a variety of new ways to consume the information that matters to them.

You likely use social media in your personal life, and perhaps even in professional settings like an internship or job. You are probably among the 73 percent of online adults using Facebook (among more than 1 billion global users) or 43 percent using multiple social sites, according to the Pew Research Center's Internet Project. Platforms such as LinkedIn, Twitter, Instagram and Pinterest may also draw your attention through a mobile device. eMarketer describes mobile trends as making users "always on, always social" through smartphones and tablets. We are used to people making mobile status updates or uploading photos while walking to class, hanging out at the gym or celebrating with friends.

Media consumption is shifting in society, impacting the ways citizens consume news and society gets informed. The Pew Research Journalism Project reports that about half of Facebook and Twitter users get news from these social sites. Reddit, Google+, YouTube, LinkedIn and Instagram also are news sources. Users may tap traditional sources too, such as print, television and radio.

News may come from "citizen journalists" who capture live events with mobile devices and then upload the information to social sites. Pew research in 2013 identified the devastating Oklahoma tornados and Boston Marathon terror attack as events that generated highly viewed citizen-captured videos on YouTube.

Blogs, now amongst the older social media forms, may also inform society and showcase citizen journalism efforts. Paul Andrews in the Nieman Report, "Is Blogging Journalism?" notes how bloggers influence traditional journalism. While blogs do not necessarily adhere to journalism reporting standards, they may interact with readers and help circulate information among readers and journalists.

Some principles or best practices help guide journalists toward integrating social and mobile tools. In a couple of years, the tools mentioned here may change, and new ones emerge. Given this reality, the focus ahead will be on the best uses and ways of infusing social media into journalism practice, no matter the exact platforms and features.

This chapter walks you through professional uses of social media for producing news in the convergence environment. After taking note of the big trends, this chapter will highlight the following three areas:

- Ways to produce news content with uses of social media.
- Using online writing, visual and social-sharing tactics to enhance news content and circulation online.
- Understanding and engaging with audiences on their chosen platforms for accessing information.

Observing Trends

Journalists once worked in a mass-media model in which they disseminated one message, via print or broadcast news, to a large audience. Online interaction ushered in with convergence has shifted this model significantly. This section of the chapter will explore the ways in which social media and an increasing reliance on digital technology have led to massive changes in how we view journalism and communication.

User-generated content

The era of Web 2.0, which Tim O'Reilly defined in 2005, marked the start of user-generated content (UGC) online. Web 2.0 transformed online interactions from push-out content from Web developers to an arena in which anyone, without a background in Web programming, could put content online.

You create UGC regularly when you post status updates on social network sites or upload pictures to photo-sharing networks. What's important to know is that when the Web shifted to a place where anyone could put content online, our interactions with information and news changed too.

For example, you can watch "The Bachelor" on prime-time television, or follow "spoiler" updates of what will happen on the show via blogs and Facebook pages. You can also use Twitter hashtags to see what other viewers think about the unfolding drama and share your thoughts as well. NBC News reports in "Game of spoilers: Social media is killing DVR culture" how this UGC disrupts live viewing by informing viewers of "what happens" before the show is seen.

Seeing consumers and producers

Thinking beyond changes for individuals, we also see UGC changing how our society functions in getting news. In "Convergence Culture", Henry Jenkins describes an emerging participatory culture in which people who were just media consumers ten years ago are now content consumers and producers. We now post updates online and engage in online sharing of information through updates, pictures and video. Social sharing has shifted each of our roles from media spectator to media participant.

With consumers who also serve as content producers, the opportunity for crowd-sourcing comes into play. Here we see the online sharing of news, pictures and opinions coming together from several types of people in various places converging in an online space. For example, innovative ideas for recycling may come from people in various U.S. states, but be gathered or sourced from this diverse "crowd" on one Twitter hashtag. Bigger ideas about happenings or trends based on patterns emerge from the massive expression of the public or "the crowd."

Using mobile devices and apps

Increasingly, our participation is mobile. Pew reported in 2013 that 55 percent of Americans own smart phones, with 91 percent owning mobile phones. Further, 32 percent owned e-readers and 42 percent owned tablets. Mobile devices use applications – software programs designed for tablets or phones – to access news, social media and

167

business sites. These apps allow easy and streamlined access to content from a mobile device. Gartner reports that 92 percent of apps downloaded in 2013 were free versions, in which users access the app in exchange for sharing their data or viewing advertising.

This exchange produces one form of "Big Data," a term for large, complex data sets, which at times is sourced through the social platforms that gather data about individual online activities. Forbes refers to Big Data as "a collection of data from traditional and digital sources inside and outside your company that represents a source for ongoing discovery and analysis."

Big Data from online activities and preferences allows companies to profile us. It shows what users like and don't like, allowing companies to serve preferred content, such as relevant news, or coupons based on consumer buying behavior. It's like going to a restaurant and only being shown items on the menu that you like. That predetermined menu increasingly influences our online experiences – news, advertising and other content. Big Data results from all that data collection and is increasingly used by companies – and even in reporting with data-driven journalism.

Seeking media uses and gratifications

Users may access news and UGC at any time to satisfy their information needs. Another way to view this is from the perspective of uses and gratifications, a theoretical view of how users decide to use forms of media. Researcher Guosong Shao describes users using media in different ways to fulfill needs for information, entertainment and mood management; for example, when users find particular forms of media easy to use and control, like reading a magazine or scrolling through a mobile newsfeed. Users can also gain fulfillment from self-expression with the content they produce online.

Think of users as gatekeepers deciding on the types of content they are interested in so they can satisfy their needs for information or entertainment – from particular sources like online news sites or on certain topics like sports, fashion, local happenings or breaking news.

Posing challenges and opportunities

Taken together, news consumers are also producers, able to access content from mobile devices in order to fulfill needs for information and entertainment. Journalists and other information creators need to think about creating content that fits this audience's needs.

Journalists must orient news production and content to fit the needs of a diverse audience, seeking multiple ways to engage with news stories. You have probably observed that print journalism has struggled to transition to this new model during the last decade. Today, news reaches audiences through multi-platform options that meet the on-demand expectations of society. The old model provided media content in one format for all. In comparison, the modern individualized model must provide media content in multiple formats – for the audiences tuning in via tablets, websites, Facebook or Twitter feeds and many other ways.

Many news organizations can now use website analytics and user data from mobile apps to gain specific insight into how particular news content is relevant or interesting for users. Journalists can now use this data to determine what readers use and what they are talking about. The journalists can then figure out how to provide the information that matters to users.

Producing News Content

169

Your interest in news is likely based on writing or visual skills. You are developing these skills in order to work as a journalistic writer or photographer or videographer. No matter your discipline, you are producing news content as a storyteller. To be an effective storyteller, social media can help you get the facts, sources and various perspectives that will help make the story accurate, objective and trustworthy. Journalists serve the public, and social media helps them interact with that public. Here are a few social media tools you can use. Keep in mind that social tools are offered as examples only, and new tools are always emerging.

Brainstorming for story writing and visuals

Turn to social media to get ideas about ways to cover an issue or major threads to national or local issues that may be relevant to your story assignment. Further, photos and videos on a variety of social sites, particularly YouTube, can show citizen journalism or corporate videos that lend insight into the topic you are covering.

Let's say your editor asks you to put together a story on the marijuana legalization issues relevant in your state and community. You may have limited knowledge of this topic, and social media could help you examine legal, medical and educational aspects of the issue.

HANGING OUT AT A "VIRTUAL" COFFEE SHOP

Think of social media as a virtual coffee shop – though immensely diverse compared to a real coffee shop, and with varying levels of formal or casual interaction.

- Facebook and Twitter, as well as public comment areas on news websites or recommendation sites like Yelp, can serve as open places for sharing about ideas, happenings and opinions.
- Inherent qualities of social media are openness and provoking conversation – and it's also a transparent channel for sharing interactions.
- Formally or casually, you can ask the audience for information to develop and verify your story.
- Your audience can interact with you regarding opinion, facts or even errors that arise.
- You can listen easily to what audiences are saying. These people may come and go at the coffee shop, while you listen, observe and contribute information to the conversation.
- Endless methods for testing and experimenting with news content and ways to cover it are available through social media. Major social sites like YouTube, Facebook, Twitter, Instagram and Pinterest are examples of places for research about issues that matter.

You could also use social media to solicit views from law enforcement and other key groups.

In addition to reading pertinent news articles, you can see how the story is being broadly discussed in YouTube searches on "marijuana legalization" or tags on Twitter or Instagram. You might find Facebook groups discussing the issue. You will likely come across a variety of voices, even though not all of them will be helpful. However, your brainstorming will expand with a quick view of multiple aspects of the topic.

Further, brainstorming and seeing others' points of view can help you determine what may be the key parts of the story to cover, further story ideas or local factors. You should also brainstorm search terms or hashtags for a particular story, and try various uses of them on several social sites.

Finding and verifying sources

The people commenting on Twitter hashtags or Facebook groups can be researched through a Google search. The search can help you find out more background on some of these voices and potentially other things the sources are saying. Another way to verify new sources is through profiles on LinkedIn, a professionally oriented social network site. These profiles typically describe a source's current job, work history and professional and interest groups.

Let's get back to the idea of a story regarding the legalization of marijuana. Social media can be useful as you seek sources on both sides of the issue. You might look for vocal community members with important beliefs about legislative action or community impacts. Researching people discussing these issues could be helpful in locating sources, verifying the credibility of these people and getting quotable information for your story.

You can also let the source know through public or private messaging that you would like to conduct an interview. You also could find the source's contact information through social media and then reach that person in a more traditional format. Either way, social media can help you know more about the source you will meet.

You can access information from a source through prior interviews or statements posted on YouTube, podcasts or other audio capture that may include video. You can use this information in your news article if the source is not available.

Follow official sources like law enforcement, companies, sports teams or public officials, who may be quotable through social media. Additionally, follow unofficial sources such as active community members or vocal power users of social sites and blogs for updates that may include breaking news that you can verify with official sources.

Checking the pulse of social conversation

Increasingly, discussion of issues important in the community happens on social media. This makes social media an ideal way to listen to what people are saying and sharing in your community. For example, regarding a complicated issue like climate change, you can monitor conversations underway among Facebook users or Twitter hashtags. Some comments may be personal opinions about climate change, and others may be factual from scientists or research groups.

It's important not to assume chatter on social media covers all aspects of an important issue or serves as a true representation of society. Just because many people are sharing opinions about climate change on social media, it doesn't mean that those people are "right." Think of the social conversation like a convenience sample – a way to get a sense of what people are thinking.

"Crowd-sourcing" information and citizen status updates for stories

You may crowd-source research or information for your story, which means tapping into networks of people regarding shared experiences, opinions or ideas. Crowd-sourcing allows you to gain access to a wide number of views and group some of those views together as a convenience sample. Individual insights also may spark ideas for broader trends or issues for your story.

Ask people related to a particular topic to chime in on designated Facebook pages or Twitter hashtags, upload pictures, leave comments on news blogs or participate in polls. Invite unique views, shared experiences and pictures to a broad array of story topics: What was it like winning the high school basketball trophy at state? Who can recall Main Street from the 1970s? What ideas could improve business in the industrial park? What priorities should the mayor address this year?

Invite citizen journalists to submit insights, conversational input, photos or video to add to local coverage. However, make sure you validate their work in order to ensure accuracy.

A good way to do this is to blend your reliable sources – like the highway department talking about bad weather conditions – with crowd-sourced insights – such as Twitter updates from motorists who reported poor highway conditions. A status update about hazardous driving may serve as a good example to back up what the highway department is saying.

A word of caution: You are still responsible for every bit of information you use and publish. To that end, not every citizen journalist will be familiar with the strictures associated with fact checking, journalism ethics and other tenets you hold dear as a professional. You should use the material you receive from crowd-sourcing, Twitter feeds and other citizen-journalism outlets with care. Make sure you are able to verify information and stand behind what you have published. (See Chapter 13 for more on the ethics associated with this kind of work.)

COVERING LIVE EVENTS WITH SOCIAL MEDIA

As a reporter, you may cover a live news event. Your coverage can involve writing a story and "live reporting" via social media while the event is underway. Readers or viewers may tune in to your live updates on social media. These tips cover planning ahead and making updates from the scene.

Before the event

- Preview the event by letting your followers know that you will be making live updates on Twitter, Facebook, Instagram and/or other platforms.
- Think ahead of certain aspects you expect to cover so you can easily provide coverage without looking up information online.
- If you look up the following information ahead of the event, you can insert these items during your live reporting:
  - Links to previous stories, pictures or Web resources, such as local history, related issues or past actions
  - References for key individuals or organizations involved, such as Twitter handles or Facebook references that you could cite in your updates
  - Twitter hashtags for key issues being discussed
- Consider using a social media management application, such as HootSuite, which allows you to easily make status updates to multiple social media accounts.

During the event

- Make regular status updates to multiple platforms like Facebook and Twitter, as well as Instagram and others that readers may tune in to.
- Follow up on your final story by posting links to the story on Twitter hashtags or Facebook.
- Quote people who speak or take action during the event, and use those quotes as live tweets or Facebook updates. This is where anticipating Twitter handles or Facebook names before the event can save you time.
- Be creative with funny or human sides of the story. For example, was there a surprise delivery of flowers or birthday celebration before the team hit the court or the council took up business? How can you show these moments?

173

- Ask questions of your audience and use real-time responses to help you understand community reaction as you write the story that will appear on your news website or publication.
- Show something from behind the scenes. For example, The Washington Post aggregated journalists' "hilarious and gross" experiences when staying in Sochi, Russia, for the 2014 Winter Olympics – complete with social media updates and pictures.

After the event

- Show screenshots of social conversations in your story, such as screenshots from social media platforms or compilations through social sites like Storify.
- View what people were saying for follow-up coverage with ongoing issues.
- Consider thanking sources or the readers who commented in responses on social media regarding your story.

174

Researching and interacting with groups

As a professional journalist, your storytelling will require you to interact with diverse groups of people, such as advocacy groups, governmental organizations and religious groups. Some of these people will be highly recognizable, while others will be new faces on the scene. Social media is another way to become informed and interactive.

Quick background information can be found at Wikipedia, though it should be used with caution and not as a source. The social site is continually updated and offers crowd-sourced information and editing – which leads to potentially good links to back up entries but also the possibility that information is not reliable. In general, citing Wikipedia is not advised. As noted in the American Journalism Review, journalists are responsible for accurate sources and must ensure them outside of Wikipedia.

Using Online Writing, Visual and Social-sharing Tactics

As users engage in more digital media, which is increasingly mobile, their attention spans tend to shorten. Some long-form news stories will draw extended spans of attention, but journalists should realize that many readers will seek quicker reads.

Decreasing attention spans put additional responsibility on the journalist to creatively capture interest and keep it long enough for users to understand the story. Journalists are also fighting with other sites for attention, sites that are using algorithm-baiting techniques to push their work higher and others lower. For example, companies often optimize websites for search engines in order to appear higher in search results. Good writing can help journalists draw readers as well as attract search engines.

Writing online to compel interest and social sharing

Readers tend to scan online information and gravitate toward shorter text. Envision audiences for your story and their platforms.

You should add copy breaks, sub-heads and bullet points to aid online reading. This approach can be challenging depending on the format expectations of your publication. Breakouts are another way to help a reader quickly see the main points of a story issue. You also want to link to sources, relevant websites and background information to support information in your article. When inserting links, think like the person reading your story. For example, a restaurant review on Google search from a mobile device could add functionality by linking to the restaurant and Yelp reviews in the story.

Compelling headlines can grab attention and views. Readers may be more likely to read a story with the headline "Toddler tests as third-grader – admitted to kindergarten" than one titled "Gifted toddler at head of class." Headlines should also include search terms in order to add relevancy for the search engines.

175

Increasing use of visuals, pictures, infographics and short video

Web and mobile platform users will likely want to see photos and view videos while they read text on their screens. This crossover of traditional broadcast and print journalism is happening online. Broadcasters are adding visuals and text to online formats while publications are adding video to online storytelling.

Our culture is becoming increasingly visual with online media, and a panel at the 2013 International Symposium on Online Journalism highlighted this topic. The panel emphasized the importance of visuals in storytelling via information graphics, interactive multimedia elements and data-backed graphical images. This convergence of print, audio, visuals and video can increase reader engagement.

You may shoot a photo or a short video at a news event. This video or picture may be posted to Facebook, Twitter, Instagram and other platforms in "real time" and also accompany your online news article.

You may alert readers ahead of the story in two ways with visuals. First, you could provide advance images on social media to preview the event. Then you could provide your audience members with pictures or video afterward to follow up. Second, depending on the topic, you might crowd-source visuals from readers. These approaches help encourage readers to watch for your updates and engage with you on social media.

With daily news coverage, brainstorm ways to add visuals. You can use screenshots independently or in a slideshow to show user-created social media updates. You also might consider adding newsroom-created visuals if you have graphics expertise or green-screen access.

VIEW FROM A PRO

DAVE WASINGER

Dave Wasinger's daily duties revolve around increasing engagement with digital readers for the Lansing State Journal and two other Gannett publications, the Battle Creek Enquirer and Port Huron Times Herald.

Wasinger's fast-paced work integrates digital and social media into the news cycle, supporting interaction with readers and pushing journalism in local online conversation about key issues. Today's news cycle incorporates readers' ideas, views and information needs in reactive and proactive efforts with new media.

"Readers are saying 'this is what we want,'" Wasinger said. "And media people are working to meet that."

For 10 years, Wasinger has worked in the Midwest as a reporter, editor and photojournalist with a digital emphasis. Prior to joining the LSJ, he was digital news editor for the Oshkosh Northwestern in Wisconsin.

Figure 10.1
Dave Wasinger.

In his current role, Wasinger oversees multimedia production for the three publications and assists in Web production. This work involves integrating video into online news stories, training reporters to shoot and edit video with iPhones, managing greenroom production and creating packages from video shots – sometimes from citizen journalists.

"One of our most widely watched videos last year was a crash on a local highway," he said.

The stunning freak truck accident with no casualties was captured in a six-second Vine video. Wasinger said he contacted the local citizen journalist via social media, and coordinated placement and voiceover for the video to accompany the news story on the LSJ website.

Wasinger serves as part of the LSJ digital team that strategizes uses of social media for news coverage and events. The team looks at ways to engage readers, such as creating hashtags prior to President Barack Obama's 2014 trip to Lansing in order to generate interest and social sharing of news, photos and video for the event. The team brainstorms crowd-sourcing opportunities, such as encouraging reader contributions of comments and photos for the "Michigander" section that features cool and little-known facts about life in the Wolverine State.

Social strategy also means thinking about how readers access news via social network sites and mobile devices, he said.

"We try to update Twitter as often as possible without being overbearing," he said.

Timing is important for social media updates, as is making information relevant to readers who are accessing news on multiple platforms. The team updates Web content, linked from social media sites coinciding with peak readership times. The team also uses real-time analytics to see how readers are accessing news and clicking on stories, photos or videos of appeal.

In the future, he expects these insights to be of high value to journalists keeping an ear to social media conversations and acting on issues that matter to readers. This effort is important, he said, as journalists and editorial teams must keep pace with digital trends of increased personalization and relevancy in online content.

"Being tuned in, we can see what people are reading and make suggestions to reporters and editors," Wasinger said. "It's another tool in our toolbox."

Promoting social sharing across platforms

Think of your news content – text, images and video – as residing on your publication's website. You can link to this news content from a status update on Facebook, Twitter, LinkedIn or Google+, or from blogging sites like Blogger and Wordpress. Further, the video may be posted on YouTube and the pictures on Instagram with relevant hashtags. Many options beyond these exist.

The Lansing State Journal promoted preview news about President Obama's 2014 trip to Michigan's capital as a basis for ongoing coverage of the event. This effort involved creating a hashtag, #ObamaMSU, prior to the event. The publication also promoted engagement on Facebook and captured relevant updates from the visit with Storify.

Figure 10.2 *Facebook screen capture.*

(COURTESY OF THE LANSING STATE JOURNAL, COPYRIGHT FEBRUARY 7, 2014)

Figure 10.3 *Facebook screen capture.*

(COURTESY OF THE LANSING STATE JOURNAL, COPYRIGHT FEBRUARY 7, 2014)

Figure 10.4 *Storify screen capture.*

(COURTESY OF THE LANSING STATE JOURNAL, COPYRIGHT FEBRUARY 7, 2014)

Figure 10.5 *Twitter screen capture and links.*
(COURTESY OF THE LANSING STATE JOURNAL, COPYRIGHT FEBRUARY 7, 2014)

Why you should care:
   https://twitter.com/LSJNews/status/431521910900285440

The anticipation/lead up to Obama's visit:
   https://twitter.com/LSJNews/status/431755249611997184

Live coverage: Cover-it Live:
   https://twitter.com/LSJNews/status/431802006773440512

Twitter list of reporters covering the visit:
   https://twitter.com/LSJNews/status/431812423478415360

Live tweets of Air Force One:
   https://twitter.com/LSJNews/status/431840347816488960
   https://twitter.com/LSJNews/status/431833042853044224
   https://twitter.com/LSJNews/status/431844983818420224
   https://twitter.com/LSJNews/status/431858271818104832

Traffic updates from motorcade:
   https://twitter.com/LSJNews/status/431849730810068992

Retweeting Obama's itinerary:
   https://twitter.com/LSJNews/status/431851041290985473

Live tweeting Obama's address:
  https://twitter.com/LSJNews/status/431872227831984128
  https://twitter.com/LSJNews/status/431870600282648576
  https://twitter.com/LSJNews/status/431874555406471169

Our most retweeted, favorited tweet (56 retweets, 15 favorites):
  https://twitter.com/LSJNews/status/431876673588314112

More traffic updates:
  https://twitter.com/LSJNews/status/431882646118203393

Air Force One taking off:
  https://twitter.com/LSJNews/status/431893718485188608

Recap and highlights:
  https://twitter.com/LSJNews/status/431992183789719552

The main idea here is that your news content can and should be linked on platforms that reach different readers. One reader may be a heavy Facebook user, while another is only on Twitter. Ideally, both of these readers would see your content on their social network site of choice. Further, as they read they may also share the link with other readers to aid information sharing within the network. This sharing behavior is considered electronic word of mouth. This sharing also is referred to at times as viral sharing or peer-to-peer sharing and can make a story very popular.

Think strategically about how the story gets to readers. Social sharing from your organization or your readers can get your story more broadly read. From those social platforms readers can access your story, and engage in social conversations around the story.

Depending on your story topic, publication and goals, it may make sense to promote your story or event coverage via viral sharing. The term viral sharing means passing along information from one user to another. Social media is a great way for social sharing to happen as readers find information interesting in a new story and then share it with "friends" or "followers" on social media platforms. This strategic approach is not a fit for every story, but the more clicks for your story, the more it has informed readers, which helps show how your story indeed "got" to readers.

Consider informing key community members or groups about your story. Community groups may be interacting with the story. For example, a story about economic issues for downtown businesses may be showing up on a Twitter hashtag or a Facebook feed from your news organization or users, as well as on LinkedIn. Readers can provide pictures from a major storm in your community that you can then share on Facebook, Twitter or YouTube. The more you can find users on their social sites, the more likely your story will be read. Increasingly, with multi-platform access, this is important.

Think about future audiences for your story too. In the future, your story may be found in a Google or social search as a reader seeks out content that you wrote. Search engines like Google keep an index of website content relevant for searches based on key words. In a sense, your article becomes archived on Google search after it runs. Consider the "after audience" that will read your story in the future.

182   Understanding and Engaging with Audiences

Many benefits await the journalist who can understand and engage audiences. Social media gives journalists an opportunity to listen to their communities in ways unimaginable a decade ago. Social media conversations provide keen insight into what readers are discussing, ways that complicated news topics affect daily lives and other helpful information for storytelling. Analytic tools on publication websites, mobile apps and social media sites also can show levels of interest for various issues and events.

In your role as a journalist, using social media is another key opportunity. You and your publication can engage with the public through your storytelling via social media. You can engage with your readers and interact with them in relation to particular stories as well as ongoing issues or events. It is important for journalists to present themselves professionally in these social interactions. You are branding yourself as an individual and potentially as a freelancer. At times you will also represent the news organization that employs you. Put your best image forward thoughtfully on social media, so you can leverage all of the benefits discussed in this chapter.

Presenting yourself as a professional journalist on social media

You should only pass along reliable information on social media. In addition, you should follow AP style, think about all the audiences that may view your updates and conduct yourself with the highest ethical standards. You need to keep a barrier between your personal social media presence and your professional social media presence. More than that, you need to understand that in some cases, the wall between these elements can break down, so you must be careful in how you approach social media in both areas.

As a professional journalist, you want to have a solid presence on LinkedIn, which is a valuable resource for connecting with sources such as politicians, business people and other community members. Use social sharing to send updates to people who you talk to for stories, as it adds to your professional presence.

Google search your name to see your digital footprint and think of managing the impressions that others form of you. Maintain high privacy settings but do not count on them to fully protect your personal information and posts.

View your online presence as a way of branding your professional self. You represent yourself, as well as your publication. Be credible and conversational with others, but show good judgment in emotional responses and humor. Your voice as a journalist is professional, not necessarily the casual, social media voice you use with your friends.

As your career progresses, you will likely change employers, but your professional online presence moves with you. It is common for employers to review the online and social media presence of potential hires. Your professionalism can help your chances of getting the job.

Clean up your non-work social media accounts. You never know when a picture or status update on a personal account may find its way to being viewed by the public or your boss. It may not sound fun, but try to be professional in all of your updates.

FINAL FOUR

If you take nothing else away from this chapter, here are four things you should remember:

1 Convergence means broad shifts for readers who are increasingly not just consumers of news but also producers. Thanks to Web 2.0 and mobile access, readers can participate in news conversations through social media. At times, they also are a source of news as reporters and editors engage with citizen journalists and crowd-sourced information.

2 In producing news content, journalists may use social media to aid story brainstorming, finding and verifying sources, crowd-sourcing comments or visuals – at times from citizen journalists – and researching new topics or organized groups. Modern storytelling involves journalists interacting with their communities. They are adding social tools into traditional journalism, which is based on accuracy, truth and objectivity.

3 Online writing needs to factor in the ways readers read text via computers or mobile devices and the importance of visual aspects to tell stories through pictures, videos and infographics. Journalists need to understand how search engines work and provide access to news stories with links and social integration. Most importantly, journalists can also promote stories across social platforms to increase readership and pass them along to others.

4 New methods for understanding audiences with social media include observing social media conversations, watching social analytics for stories and visuals of higher appeal and checking website analytics to see times and types of access for readers. Focus on engaging with your audience on social platforms. Interacting on issues with sources and community members can improve your knowledge while demonstrating professionalism and your personal "brand" as a journalist.

References

Andrews, P. (2003). "Is blogging journalism?" Nieman Reports. Retrieved from: www.nieman.harvard.edu/reportsitem.aspx?id=101027

Arthur, L. (2013). "What is big data?" Forbes.com. August 13. Retrieved from: www.forbes.com/sites/lisaarthur/2013/08/15/what-is-big-data/

Brenner, J. (2013). "Mobile Technology Factsheet." Pew Internet. September 18. Retrieved from: http://pewinternet.org/Commentary/2012/February/Pew-Internet-Mobile.aspx

Cutts, M. (n. d.). "How Search Works." Google video on YouTube. Retrieved from: www.youtube.com/watch?v=BNHR6IQJGZs

Dewey, C. (2014). "Journalists at Sochi are live-tweeting their hilarious and gross hotel experiences." *The Washington Post.* February 4. Retrieved from: www.washingtonpost.com/blogs/worldviews/wp/2014/02/04/journalists-at-sochi-are-live-tweeting-their-hilarious-and-gross-hotel-experiences/

Duggan, M., & Smith, A. (2013). "Social Media Update 2013." Pew Research Center. December 30. Retrieved from: www.pewinternet.org/Reports/2013/Social-Media-Update/Main-Findings.aspx

Holcomb, J., Gottfried, J., & Mitchell, A. (2013). "News use across social media platforms." Pew Research Center. November 14. Retrieved from: www.journalism.org/2013/11/14/news-use-across-social-media-platforms/

Jurkowitz, M. & Hitlin, P. (2013). "Citizen eyewitnesses provide majority of top online news videos in Oklahoma tornado disaster." Pew Research Center. Retrieved from: www.pewresearch.org/fact-tank/2013/05/22/citizen-eyewitnesses-provide-majority-of-top-online-news-videos-in-oklahoma-tornado-disaster/

O'Reilly, T. (2005). "What is Web 2.0." Retrieved from: http://oreilly.com/web2/archive/what-is-web-20.html

Shao, G. (2009). "Understanding the appeal of user-generated media: a uses and gratification perspective." *Internet Research, 19*(1), 7–25.

Shaw, D. (2008). "Wikipedia in the Newsroom." *American Journalism Review.* February/March. Retrieved from: http://ajrarchive.org/article.asp?id=4461

Multimedia Journalism

Steven Chappell

WANTED – MULTIMEDIA JOURNALIST

Meredith Corporation – Fairway, Kansas

The Multimedia Journalist enterprises, researches, writes, shoots, edits and reports news-oriented material for presentation live and on tape. The position collaborates with the assignment desk, producers, and managers on story development and story execution. Must also be able to operate ENG microwave truck.

Essential Job Functions:

60 percent: Shooting, writing, editing
30 percent: Story enterprise and development
10 percent: Operating ENG microwave truck
Minimum Qualifications (all must be met to be considered):

Education:

- Bachelor's degree in Broadcast Journalism, Communications or related field. Equivalent training and/or experience will be considered.

Experience:

- One to three years of reporting broadcast journalism.
- One to two years of experience shooting.
- At least two years of reporting news at a commercial television station is preferred, but internships and student media experience will be considered.

Specific Knowledge, Skills and Abilities:

- Strong writing, editing and shooting skills
- Good news gathering skills
- Strong interpersonal skills
- Attention to detail
- Ability to work in a team-oriented environment
- Strong on-air presence
- Must possess a valid driver's license
- Experience with Avid and Inews preferred
- Proficiency with MS Office
- Ability to work under tight deadlines

Introduction

As the founder of the Twitter feed @comminternships, I post daily internship and entry-level job descriptions like the one above for students such as you. This particular job description crossed my desk in early January 2014, and it was rather surprising in its detail and depth of requirements – not the least of which was the requirement that you should be able to drive and operate an ENG microwave truck, which in some states means you need a commercial driver's license.

Various authors in various chapters of this book have already addressed the host of individual skills you should acquire as part of your trek through your journalism program. This chapter will address how those skills come together, making them effective for you as you move into working as a journalist.

While the job description from Meredith Corporation isn't typical of every multimedia job, many of the skills it lists are universal. It is of benefit to you to develop as many skills as possible, but you should focus on those skills that are seen as universal. These skills include effective communication and critical thinking.

If you graduate with a specific set of technical skills, then you have demonstrated to employers that you have the ability to learn and adapt. The technical skills you are learning today will likely evolve, change and possibly cease to exist altogether by the time you enter the job market.

I'm speaking from experience: My technical skills upon earning my undergraduate degree included being adept with a typewriter, pica pole, X-acto knife, proportion wheel and a waxer (I'll let you practice your reporting skills and Google that term). If those items are in a newsroom today, they are typically in a history collection.

However, that doesn't mean you shouldn't focus on the technical skills of today and master them to the best of your ability. Pretty much every new technology evolves from something that came before it. For example, Twitter, in some ways, is just a shorter way to make a Facebook post. While certain forms of technology may eventually become obsolete, knowing it now may be the key to you getting the job instead of the student sitting at the desk behind you.

Getting Started in Skill Development

So, what specific multimedia skills do you need? It depends on whom you ask, and what job you seek, but the basics seem to be ubiquitous. In addition to strong writing and newsgathering skills, you should have knowledge of solid photography (still and video) techniques and audio editing skills. You also want to be proficient at mobile-based reporting, which includes social media, blogging and search engine optimization (SEO). Some knowledge of basic coding will also help you.

You have to be able to multitask, and that means you need to be effective at time management. With any luck, you will have a multimedia editor or director back in the newsroom guiding you along, but you can't depend on that.

What the pros are doing

Steve Booher, multimedia news editor of newspressnow.com (which is a melding of the St. Joseph News-Press, Fox 26 KNPN and News-Press 3 Now), frequently gives talks to college student journalists about what he wants when students apply to work for him. He says the talk changes every year, as it did in late 2013 when he spoke to a group of advanced reporting students from Northwest Missouri State University.

"We reinvent ourselves every day," Booher said. "The days of the hardnosed newspaper reporter are gone. You are going to have to do a whole bunch of other things."

189

MULTIMEDIA TOOLS FOR TODAY

As newspressnow.com City Government Reporter Kim Norvell explains later in this chapter, you have to have a diverse tool set. Her reporting bag always contains:

- A smartphone, which has:
* Spare charger cables (and even an external battery pack).
* A solid Twitter app for making quick posts from the story location.
* An audio recorder (she uses the Voice Memos app that comes preinstalled).
* A good video app (she just uses the iPhone camera, but if you can afford it and have the space, I recommend FILMiC Pro).
* A good notes program (Evernote is a good choice).
- An old-fashioned reporter's notebook as well as pens and pencils (technology breaks, remember?).

Also, it doesn't hurt to own and plan to use:

- A laptop or solid tablet computer for writing the story and editing audio and video.
- A good digital SLR that also captures HD video.
- A decent digital audio recorder, as a backup when the smartphone battery dies or when the smartphone is needed for other work, like live tweets and blog updates.

Getting started quick tips

- Know how to operate a smart phone. Make certain its camera is capable of shooting high-quality still photos and HD video.
- Be prepared to adapt – both on assignment and in the job. As Booher said: "We reinvent ourselves every day."
- Diversify your skill set. Take classes in audio, still photography, video and print. Take every writing and editing class you can. Since you are likely going to appear on camera, take some public speaking classes.
- Learn to code, even if it's just basic HTML. Learning the basics of the language will help you adapt later, if it's necessary.
- Get some practical experience. This may be the media adviser in me talking, but working for student media is the best starting point for every journalism major.

In the case of newspressnow.com City Government Reporter Kim Norvell, photographers and videographers are still part of the mix, but she said she often has to fill several roles during breaking news situations.

"I take my phone and notebook, and I record audio and tweet and use my reporter's notebook," Norvell said. "I'll shoot video or take photos on my phone, too, but when that's planned a photographer or videographer usually goes with me."

How to Get Going

Today's media environment developed over time, and some of it happened because of traditional media's blindness to the changing landscapes. Tim Stephens, deputy managing editor at CBS Interactive and president of the Associated Press Sports Editors (APSE), said his observations from his time as a traditional print journalist have led him to many of the same conclusions as Booher.

"What we're trying to change and what I'm beating people with is 'think like the user,'" Stephens said. "You can't do it the way everyone's done it."

191

Stephens said this applies to student media as well. He said students are learning some of the skills they need to succeed, but they aren't applying them properly in their student newsrooms.

"Stop tinkering with your content," Stephens said. "The surest way to fail is to be a newspaper online. You are guaranteed to suck."

Stephens worked as a traditional print reporter and editor for 20 years before going multimedia and said he had to change his perspective on everything in news.

"I've had to change my thinking entirely," Stephens said. "The hardest part of this leadership process is getting people to let go of the paper. It doesn't matter. Your job is not to matter about where it goes. It's to produce the content."

For Stephens, the traditional "gatekeeper" concept of news is out the window. To succeed in the industry today, it's not about giving users what you think they need. It's about giving them what they want.

"You can't do it the way everyone's done it: Take a weak, declining product and put it online and call it a newspaper online and then take that content and turn it into mobile content," Stephens said. "You have to know what your audience wants."

VIEW FROM A PRO

TIM STEPHENS

Tim Stephens is the deputy managing editor at CBSSports.com and the president of the Associated Press Sports Editors for 2013–14. At CBS, Stephens shapes the website's daily news content while supervising three assistant managing editors and all of the newsroom's writing staff. He also directs the staff's investigative and project reporting efforts and collaborates with CBS Sports, CBS Sports Network, CBS Sports Radio and local CBS affiliates.

Figure 11.1
Tim Stephens.

Before joining CBS in 2012, Stephens led award-winning sports departments at the Orlando Sentinel, South Florida Sun Sentinel and the Birmingham (Alabama) Post-Herald. He's hired hundreds of newly-minted journalists in his career. Here's what it takes for him to notice your résumé:

1 Compete for the job. Remember that the job search is not about you – it's about the hirer. Don't rehash the resume in your cover letter. I can read. Spin that resume forward. Show me how those experiences relate to the job you're seeking. Put yourself in the job. Use the cover letter to show that you know what the company you're applying to is about and how what you're about can fit in and help them. Don't send the same letter you sent 27 other places. Personalize, personalize, personalize. I've never met anyone named "Hiring Manager." Do some research and find out who needs to get the letter. A cover letter can tell me a lot about an applicant . . . subtle and sometimes not-so-subtle clues about how they compete, how they communicate, how they prepare, how they research, how interested they really are in the opening, how much they pay attention to detail. A good cover letter can get you into the game, but the resume, clips and interview seal the deal.

2 Diversify your skills set. Newsrooms are smaller and leaner. They need people who can do it all, even in the largest news organizations. Video, photos, SEO, programming, writing, editing, social media – get experience in all areas. Be proficient and efficient in storytelling across all platforms, using all of the tools available.

3 Have a specialty. Yes, you need to be able to do everything well, but if you have a specialty, it can separate you from the pack, especially if you have a skill or a knowledge base that is uncommon or in high demand.

4 Remember the fundamentals. Yes, you need to understand how to apply SEO. Yes, you need to be able to shoot, edit and post your own video stories if necessary. These things are not useful if you are not a strong reporter. Don't dare leave college without gaining an exceptional understanding of how to use public records to obtain basic information, without knowing how to interpret a financial spreadsheet for news value or how to hone your interview skills in a way that leads to intelligent, effective follow-up questions. As a reporter, you are only as good as the information you can obtain.

5 Don't be an idiot. If you do dumb things on social media, I will find it. And I will hold it against you with extreme prejudice.

As a hiring manager, I am attaching my reputation to yours when I move you through the stack.

Stephens said that today's traditional media consumers are "dying off," and for media to reach younger audiences, it must think and act like them. As a budding journalist, you are best equipped to lead media into a new age of journalism.

"Your readership is moving to two places: Their phone, and the casket," Stephens said. "[Today's media] have digital urgency. You have to be a digital ninja."

MUST-HAVE SOCIAL MEDIA ACCOUNTS

When speaking to the professional journalists for this chapter, each had his or her own idea of what social media accounts a budding multimedia journalist should have and use to get noticed. However, the group generally agreed on five online basics:

- A Twitter account. Your account profile should explain why you are on Twitter in terms an employer will understand and respect. It should be professional, but also conversational and engaging. It can have personal material, but keep it clean. Above all, don't lock your Twitter account. If you do, it serves no professional purpose.

- A Facebook page. This one had some disagreement, because some of the reporters felt it was perfectly fine to have a closed, purely personal Facebook account, but editors felt differently. This account should be used, editors say, to push your friends and followers to your online work. Remember, it's all about the eyeballs.

- A website. You should, by now, have your own domain name. If you don't, buy it before you finish reading this chapter. You need to have an online home to showcase your work. This will be the home of your professional portfolio, and the domain shouldn't end in "blogspot" or "wordpress," it should be your name, if at all possible.

- A YouTube account/channel. If you are shooting video or recording audio, this is where you house it.

- An Instagram or other photo service account. Again, you need somewhere to house all those great news, feature and sports photos you are taking for your work, as a student media member or intern.

Putting skills to the test

Jesse Stewart, a 2013 graduate of Simpson College, a small, private liberal arts college in Indianola, Iowa, spent much of his college career focused on radio. He ran the campus radio station for three years, and he turned that experience into his first real-world gig as the farm director at Three Eagles Communications, a radio group in northern Iowa.

Stewart said most of his time is spent going on the air before dawn, providing farm and local news updates. Rarely is the farm director expected to deal with breaking news or work across multiple platforms. However, he was grateful for that training in the winter of 2014, when a local fertilizer plant exploded, precipitating the evacuation of one of the towns in his coverage area. To complicate matters, the explosion occurred during a blizzard, and he was the only person in the studio. As he said,

> It was supposed to be a simple day. All I was supposed to do was run the board while our sports and news directors were covering the state wrestling tournament in Des Moines. But when this happened, I was it. I was updating the five Facebook pages (one for each radio station in the broadcast group), Twitter feeds and doing live breaking news reports all afternoon. I was thankful for the cross-training I received with my multimedia journalism degree. If I had just focused on radio, I never would have been ready for that day.

Every story you cover is a competition, Stephens said. It's a competition not to be the first to get the story, though that may be a part of it. It's more of a competition to tell the story in a way that will be compelling to your digital consumers. It's also a competition to impress the search engines that will push your content to the top of the search results.

As Stephens said,

> Keywords, SEO (search engine optimization; break out box provides details) fields, first 150 words, byline, paper's name or company's name, links within story, photos, captions, keywords, alt text, video, description of the video, the alt-text behind the video, the collection within the collection, on the rank of said collection, on the relates, of the relates of the relates, of your archives, search engine and social media. And you do this with every piece of content on your website. Every piece of content on your website is a competition for eyeballs. And if you don't, you are irrelevant.

Although larger media organizations will have people helping with the delivery, smaller organizations might not. Even larger ones expect some level of competence across the board. Stephens works for CBS Sports, and these are the skills he seeks when he hires new journalists for his operation. You aren't just a journalist. You're a competitor.

"You can't work for me if you can't compete," Stephens said. "If you can't bring a competitive mentality to every level of the story, you won't find an audience."

195

GETTING GOING QUICK TIPS

- Be ready for change. Don't expect what you learn and do today will exist tomorrow.

- Think like the consumer. How do you want to consume news and information? Learn how your target audience wants to consume news and information, and deliver it that way.

- Don't just learn *how* those consumers want their information, learn *what* information is important to them.

- Be a ninja. Don't think simple journalism skills will cut it. You have to be digitally savvy as well. Know how search engine optimization works, and learn all the tips and tricks behind it.

- Be a competitor. If you aren't, someone else will beat you.

How to Get Ahead

This may seem overwhelming to you. You might be asking yourself right now, "Why did I want to be a journalist again? This seems like a lot of work!" That's true. But remember, pretty much every industry is undergoing a technological revolution right now. Some are happening at different speeds, and some are happening at different times, but it's happening everywhere.

What makes journalism different is that the job changes every day. Today's story may be about a farm auction, and tomorrow's may be about a tornado that wipes out a town. You never know what's going to happen from day to day in terms of the news. You also never know what's going to happen from day to day in terms of the technology.

Despite all of the technology that's been thrown at you through this book and this chapter, one thing still matters: Telling the story.

"Define yourself by storytelling and information, not the delivery system," Stephens said. "If you can do that, you will be relevant to your reader and to your audience."

It's not all about the tools

Booher went so far as to say technical skills don't sell him a good employee. It's the ability to write well, and learn on the job.

"We're not hiring for people who have every technical skill," he said. "We're hiring people who have the ability to learn and adapt, and who can tell a compelling story."

A recent survey supports Booher's statement. According to a Poynter Institute survey, a gap exists between journalism educators and professionals regarding the importance of digital skills. Journalism educators tend to place more emphasis on the importance of technical skills than do media professionals, by a fairly wide margin.

That doesn't mean you should abandon learning the technical skills, but it does mean you need to ensure you have a firm grasp on essential reporting and writing skills.

Build your brand, establish your credentials

To be employed as a multimedia journalist, you will need a digital portfolio and resume – a website that showcases your storytelling abilities across multiple platforms. It will need also need to link to your social media sites and anything else online that sells you not just as a journalist, but also as a brand.

The brand is the component that sells your ability to learn and adapt. Ideally, you will have been active as a multimedia journalist through your coursework, student media employment and internships before you start looking for that first job outside of college. Your brand will be everything you have done as a multimedia journalist up to this point. It needs to demonstrate proficiency in every basic journalistic skill, and mastery of a subset of those skills, to get you noticed by potential employers.

That's the path Tiffany Gibson, who graduated from Middle Tennessee State University in 2011, took to her current position as news and Web editor for NewsOK, the online component of The Oklahoman. Gibson built her online brand from scratch at a time when her college professors and student newspaper colleagues were just beginning to realize a brand's value.

"I didn't have much professional training or instruction on how to do that in the classroom or even in my newsroom," Gibson said. "We were just learning what Twitter was and how to use Facebook beyond posting photos from frat parties when I started out as a college journalist, but I decided I wanted to do more."

Gibson took it upon herself to learn how to shoot video, record audio and produce multimedia packages for her student newspaper website. When an opportunity arose to apply for a multimedia internship with the Las Vegas Sun, Gibson decided it was an opportunity she couldn't pass up. She said,

> It was a big gamble and a big risk. I had no idea if I would get the internship. It was a competitive process. I had to produce a story on a short deadline for them, but I got it. I was the only intern selected who wasn't from some major university with a famous journalism school. I was told by the editor I got the internship because of my entrepreneurship of learning the tools on my own.

Gibson eventually landed in Oklahoma, where she now handles digital content for NewsOK.com. Her tasks include managing all of the site's social media feeds as well as producing multimedia content for the site.

"I never would have landed this job without my college experience," Gibson said. "It let me learn and try new things and figure it all out. My digital portfolio is the most valuable thing I gained from college."

Your digital resume will be far more than just that traditional list of prior employers and what you did on the job. It will be a living history with tweets, Facebook posts, Instagram images, Vine videos,

YouTube videos, blogs and whatever else you may have used as part of your work.

Just remember: Keep your social media work that also doubles as professional accounts clean. That doesn't mean they have to be free of your personal life, but they shouldn't contain anything that could keep you from getting hired for any job.

SOCIAL MEDIA AND YOU

If you have multiple social media accounts, but some of them may have displayed, shall we say, some of your less savory talents, you should delve into your social media history.

Every social media platform lets you do this. Facebook has recently unveiled its own history tool that lets you see every single thing you have ever posted – or had posted about you – on the site. Learn what's out there about you, and take the time to clean it up. Delete anything that raises questions about you. It will likely still be archived somewhere, but you should still be proactive and take care of as much of it as you can.

Social media have made your life far less private, but these tools also have made your abilities as a multimedia journalist far more public. Several employers who frequently post through @comminternships told me that it's a person's work outside their portfolio that helped someone land the job as much as what was formally presented to the employer.

This means you need to be diligent, and be cognizant that every post you make online may eventually be considered a part of your future application process. It's a frightening, and daunting, challenge, but it's also the reality of today's media market.

FINAL FOUR

If you take nothing else away from this chapter, here are four things you should remember:

1 Master the basics. Good reporting is still good reporting, regardless of the platform. Master writing skills (and this includes grammar and AP Style). Learn how to tell a good story. Learn the basic tools inside and out.

2 Think like a user. Today's media is about the consumer much more than it is about you, the journalist. Don't just deliver content to the user. Deliver that content in ways and on platforms that consumers use.

3 Be a ninja. Don't just learn the lingo, you also need to understand how it works. Be ready to produce content that has strong SEO qualities, and that may mean taking a computer class or two. In automotive terms, it means not just knowing that turning the key cranks the car, it means knowing how everything under the hood works, too. You are going to have to become technologically proficient.

4 Evolve and adapt. When new technology emerges, learn it and figure out how it works, and how you can make it work for you – and your consumers. Stay ahead of the game. Don't just sit back and watch it unfold. Unfold it for yourself. If you are going to compete for eyeballs and for jobs, you have to be ahead of everyone else in every stage of the game.

References

"Digital Skills Less Important to Professionals than to Educators, New Poynter Survey Shows." (2014). Retrieved from: www.prnewswire.com/news-releases/new-research-shows-wide-gap-between-professionals-and-educators-on-core-journalism-skills-254555761.html

The Law and Convergent Journalism

Daxton R. "Chip" Stewart

Introduction

As technological changes redefine and disrupt the practice of journalism, one thing remains constant: Every time you publish something, you take on the risk of being legally responsible for any harm you cause.

Journalists can cause harm in a number of ways: Defamation, invasion of privacy and infringement of intellectual property rights to name a few. These potential risks – and some tips on how to avoid them – are the focus of this chapter.

The law is not all about danger zones and liability for journalists. American law enables widespread freedom to publish through the First Amendment's guarantees that largely protect speech and press from government interference. Similarly, state and federal law provide some rights that help journalists do their jobs. For example, open meetings laws allow access to government activities, and reporter shield laws can protect journalists' confidential sources. The implications of these laws are also discussed in this chapter.

The First Amendment

> Congress shall make no law respecting an establishment of religion, or prohibiting the free exercise thereof; or abridging the freedom of speech, or of the press; or the right of the people peaceably to assemble, and to petition the government for a redress of grievances.
>
> (First Amendment of the U.S. Constitution)

These 45 words are the foundation of journalism in the United States, as they provide liberty from government restraint on speaking and publishing. However, the amendment doesn't provide absolute protection for all acts of journalism. Centuries of legal wrangling have made it clear that the phrase "Congress shall make no law ... abridging freedom of speech, or of the press" is quite pliable.

For example, the First Amendment only applies to actions of the state. While the word "Congress" has now been extended to all government bodies, this does not mean private groups cannot limit or punish actions of speech or the press. Businesses, private universities and professional sports leagues may take actions restricting speech and the press.

Also, the words "no law" do not actually mean *no* law. The First Amendment does not protect several kinds of speech or expressive conduct, including obscenity, true threats, false advertising and fighting words. The press clause makes it difficult for the government to prevent publication through injunctions and gag orders. It also allows for the coverage of trials and the publication of leaked government documents such as the Pentagon Papers and diplomatic records posted on Wikileaks, for example. However, in one famous case that settled before it reached the Supreme Court (United States vs. The Progressive, decided by a federal district court in Wisconsin in 1979), the government successfully prevented a magazine from publishing an issue on how to build a hydrogen bomb.

The laws outlined in this chapter – defamation, privacy restrictions, copyright – are generally exceptions that courts have allowed to coexist with the great freedoms provided by the First Amendment.

Defamation

Defamation is speaking or publishing false statements that harm another person. While there are various potential tort actions for this – for example, libel for the printed word, slander for the spoken word

– American law generally treats these harms similarly. If you say false things that hurt another person's reputation and cause them financial or emotional harm, you can be held responsible in court.

In general, the First Amendment does not protect publishers from the harms they cause to private citizens or businesses. The Media Law Resource Center released a study in 2012, finding that of the nearly 600 cases involving media defendants it had tracked since 1980, most of them exclusively involved defamation. In those cases, the plaintiffs – that is, the people suing media for damages caused by publication – won about 60 percent of the time, with an average judgment of $2.86 million. A handful of large verdicts skewed that number, and several of the judgments were overturned on appeal, but defamation remains a serious danger to journalists.

To avoid defamation cases, journalists should have an understanding of how the law operates. Each state has its own interpretation of what constitutes libel, but statutes and the common law across the United States are consistent enough to provide this as a functional definition:

> Libel is publication of a false and defamatory statement of fact that causes harm and is made with a certain level of awareness or neglect.

203

Let's explore each of these elements individually:

Publication

Typically, defamation involves publication to at least one other person besides the publisher and the person claiming harm. In this sense, publication is the easiest thing for a plaintiff to prove. Publication can be spoken aloud in the presence of another person, written in a letter, posted on a telephone pole, printed in a newspaper or magazine, aired in a television or radio broadcast or included in a blog or social media post on the Internet. The message does not need to be widespread, though the further the message reaches, the greater the potential damages may be.

A key thing to remember about publication is that it also includes republication, which is the repeating of other people's words. Defamation law generally makes the repeater of a libelous statement responsible for that statement as well. Thus, it is not a defense to libel to argue that you were accurately repeating someone else's quote or article. With only a few exceptions, such as online statements protected under the Communications Decency Act and privileged statements, you are responsible for what you publish.

Falsity

The statement must be false to be actionable. Additionally, in American law, the burden is typically on the plaintiff to establish the falsity of the statement. In several other countries, such as Great Britain and Australia, the courts require the publisher to prove that the statement is true. While this may seem like a small matter, it's actually a big procedural advantage for publishers in the United States. Even then, harmless falsehoods or minor errors typically do not automatically trigger damage awards. If mistakes are made, publishers can usually overcome them if they prove that the statements were "substantially true," meaning that the core aspects of the statements were truthful even if minor details were false.

Defamatory

The statement has to harm the plaintiff's reputation somehow. A statement is "libelous per se" if it includes accusations of criminal behavior, business misconduct, sexual misconduct or having a "loathsome disease," such as a sexually transmitted disease or HIV/AIDS. Other statements may also be libelous, depending on the context and circumstances under which they are made. It is not a crime, for example, to have an extensive collection of My Little Pony toys or to write "Saw" fan fiction, but if these allegations are false and made against a candidate for a U.S. Senate seat, she could establish that these falsehoods harmed her electability.

Statement of fact

Opinions are constitutionally protected, as are satire and parody. To be actionable as defamation, the statement must be one of objectively provable fact. The burden is then on the person seeking damages to establish that the statement of fact is false and hurtful.

Sometimes, statements are a mix of fact and opinion. In those circumstances, courts typically allow juries to decide whether the factual portion of the speech can be separated out into a defamatory statement. For example, a reporter stating, "This pizza is the worst thing I've ever eaten," is clearly providing an opinion. A reporter who writes, "This pizza is the worst thing I've ever seen because it has four cockroaches crawling on it," has included a statement of fact that could be proved or disproved objectively.

DANGER WORDS

Take care when publishing any potentially harmful allegations. This box contains a list of "danger words" that should raise extra scrutiny before you choose to publish them.

Abused, abuser	Drinking, drunk, drunken	Murdered
Addiction	Drug problem	Perjury
Adultery	Embezzled	Prostitute, prostitution
Affair	Fraud or fraudulent	Rioted
AIDS	Gay	Robbed, robbery
Alcoholism, alcoholic	Harass, harassment	Scandal
Arrested	HIV	Sex, sexual
Assaulted	Homosexual	Sexually transmitted
Attacked	Illegal	disease
Bankrupt, bankruptcy	Illicit	Slept with
Beat	Ill, illness	Smuggled
Bisexual	Immoral	Spied
Burglary	Infringed	Steal, stole, stolen
Came out of the closet	Killed	Theft
Charged	Lesbian	Trespassed
Cheat, cheated	Lied	Underage
Convicted	Mismanaged	Waste, wasted
Cover up	Mistreat	
Deviate, deviant	Molested	

Harm

To win a libel lawsuit, the plaintiff has to prove that he or she was harmed somehow. These can be "actual damages" such as lost wages because the person lost a job connected to the libelous publication, emotional suffering or other long-term reputational harm. For a company bringing a libel lawsuit, damages could include loss of stock price or other business losses caused by the defamatory statement.

It is not enough for plaintiffs to ask juries to presume that they have been harmed by offensive statements. The burden is on the plaintiff to establish exactly what that harm is.

Additionally, plaintiffs can seek "punitive damages," which judges or juries may assess to punish the bad behavior of publishers. Courts usually assess these damages against publishers who are deemed to have acted with high levels of negligence or malice in causing the harm. When multimillion-dollar damage awards happen in libel cases, it is most often because of these punitive damages, as the Media Law Resource Center has found.

Awareness

To win a defamation case, plaintiffs usually have to do more than show that something harmful and false was said about them. To protect open debate in the "marketplace of ideas," courts generally require that the plaintiff also proves that the publisher made the false statements with some sort of awareness.

For private citizens who file libel actions, the level of awareness one needs to prove is generally "negligence" – that is, that the publisher did not act with the level of care that a reasonable person would have in that circumstance. In essence, this requires journalists to act with prudence and diligence. If journalists can establish that they acted as a reasonable person would have in the same circumstances, they might prevail.

For public figures and public officials, the First Amendment requires that plaintiffs prove a higher level of awareness. In the New York Times vs. Sullivan case, the Supreme Court established that elected public officials must prove "actual malice" – that is, knowledge of falsity or reckless disregard for the truth – to prevail in a libel action. As Justice William Brennan wrote in that famous opinion, this requirement gives adequate "breathing space" for the publication of accidental falsehood to support the "profound national commitment to the principle that debate on public issues should be uninhibited, robust, and wide-open."

In essence, this makes it harder for public officials (and, after a series of court opinions after Sullivan, public figures such as celebrities) to win defamation lawsuits unless they can prove that publishers either (a) knew what they were publishing was actually false, or (b) acted with a level of journalistic malpractice – such as ignoring contrary evidence, not checking with information easily accessible to the public or refusing to interview sources that may contradict the assertions.

Defenses

The easiest way to avoid defamation is accuracy. Truth is an absolute defense in defamation cases. If the plaintiff cannot prove that the harmful assertions made are false, then the publisher wins.

Other defenses include:

- Absolute privilege, which involves accurately reporting statements made in certain places such as sworn testimonies or affidavits, statements in open court and statements made on the floor of Congress.
- "Fair report privilege," which is available in many states, protects journalists who repeat statements made in public meetings or in government records as long as they were accurately reported.
- The wire service defense can be used if you republish something that came to you through a subscription service and turned out to be untrue, as long as you didn't ignore the service's updates or corrections to those statements.
- The Communications Decency Act (CDA) protects Web forums and other interactive computer services from libel actions for items that users post in those forums. This is why news organizations are not responsible for defamatory statements that users make, even if the users themselves are liable for making the statement in the first place. Similarly, because users of these services are also protected under the CDA, people who share or retweet libelous statements also receive protection, but the original author of the statements does not.

Anti-SLAPP protection

As this section should have made clear by now, you take on the risk of defamation actions every time you publish something. Unfortunately for journalists, this means that if you publish something potentially harmful, even if you are convinced it's accurate and have substantial proof in hand, an angry person might still drag you into court.

About half of the states have recognized some kind of law to protect citizens from people who file meritless libel lawsuits. Such lawsuits, which are usually brought to silence critics, have become known as Strategic Lawsuits Against Public Participation, or SLAPPs. In turn, the laws that governmental bodies have passed to defend against these suits are known as anti-SLAPP laws.

In a typical anti-SLAPP case, a person who has been sued for defamation can ask a court to conduct an early hearing to determine if the case has any merit. If the publisher can establish that the lawsuit was brought with no chance of merit, and if the jurisdiction recognizes anti-SLAPP measures, then the court will dismiss the case. Further, the court may force the misguided plaintiff to pay damages and attorney fees to the publisher.

These laws have been tracked by the Public Participation Project at www.anti-slapp.org, where you can find out what kind of protection your state offers in these matters.

Privacy

Sometimes, a person's issue with something a journalist publishes is not that it was false, but that nobody has any right to know about the subject. In these instances, the matter at hand is privacy, not defamation. While the First Amendment generally protects the publication of truthful facts in the public interest, the law also respects certain parts of people's lives from intrusion.

Embarrassing private facts

Privacy law recognizes a tort sometimes known as "public disclosure of embarrassing private facts," which involves revealing personal information such as sexual or medical matters about people which are not a matter of public concern. While journalists generally shouldn't have any interest in writing about such matters, a jury could find something not to be as newsworthy or in the public interest as a journalist may believe. For example, publishing a person's health or illness information, sexual matters or the contents of private letters may be enough to violate the reasonable expectation of privacy of a non-newsworthy person. The key defense for publishing anything in this area is newsworthiness. If the person is a celebrity or public official and the publication relates to his or her public role or duties, the publisher is unlikely to lose.

Trespassing

Journalists have no special rights to go on private property to collect information, regardless of the public interest in it. Climbing a fence or opening a closed door at a home or business are clearly violations of trespassing law and can result in criminal charges. Any information gathered while trespassing will serve as evidence of the criminal conduct.

Trespassing may also be established if a property owner asks you to leave and you refuse. If you are on private property such as a grocery store, a shopping mall or even a parking lot, and you are behaving in a way that the owner deems inappropriate, you may be asked to leave. Journalists should be cautious and negotiate access in advance to such places before going there to take photographs or interview sources.

Intrusion

People also have some "reasonable expectation of privacy," as it has become known, from electronic or technological surveillance. Invading privacy through technological means is called "intrusion" and presents challenges for journalists.

Typically, the law says people do not have an expectation of privacy when they are in public places. However, they do have some expectation of privacy from surveillance that is beyond the usual scope of the general public. For example, using shotgun microphones, hidden cameras or other devices may violate that person's reasonable expectation of privacy. Also, states and the federal government currently make it difficult for journalists to use "unmanned aerial vehicles" such as drones to record and gather information. Federal Aviation Administration guidelines, for example, forbid using drones for commercial purposes, including journalism.

Similarly, some jurisdictions require that people be informed that they are being recorded, either through audio or video technology. Most states are "one-party consent," which means only one party to a conversation must be informed that it is being recorded, while 12 states as of early 2014 require that all parties to a conversation be aware that it is being recorded, according to the Digital Media Law Project (www.dmlp.org). Third-party surveillance, or wiretapping, is illegal under federal law and in all 50 states.

When possible, journalists should act transparently and receive consent to record or take photographs, even in public places. Journalists should also remember that they have a right to be in public places and to do their jobs without interference or harassment by the government or law enforcement. Just like any other citizen, journalists receive protection under the Fourth Amendment to the U.S. Constitution. This amendment requires the government to obtain a warrant based on probable cause of commission of a crime to search one's property or to seize evidence.

209

Confidential sources

Courts or investigators seeking to use the source material of journalism may use the subpoena process to order reporters to testify about their sources or to turn over evidence to be used in a criminal prosecution. If you ever receive a subpoena, you should not ignore it. If you fail to comply with a court order, you will likely wind up in jail for contempt of court.

However, journalists have some legal protection from such intrusion into their work. These protections are known as "reporter's privilege" or sometimes as "reporter shield laws," recognizing that sometimes journalists must grant sources confidentiality in order to protect whistleblowers who fear for their jobs or their safety if their role becomes public.

The Supreme Court, in its ruling in Branzburg vs. Hayes in 1972, only went so far as to say that "newsgathering is not without its First Amendment protections." In that case, journalists asked to be shielded from having to testify about some of their confidential sources involved in stories about illegal drugs and the Black Panthers. Federal courts have so far declined to recognize a full reporter shield based on the First Amendment, and several efforts supported by journalists to have Congress pass a law recognizing such a shield have failed.

That said, more than 30 states have extended some kind of shield to prevent journalists from having to supply evidence or testify about confidential sources. These laws generally require that the government must establish that there is no other way to get this information and that it is of critical importance to public safety and security, before it can compel journalistic cooperation. The Reporters Committee for Freedom of the Press has catalogued these efforts at www.rcfp.org/reporters-privilege.

Some jurisdictions have used similar logic to extend these protections to anonymous commenters on websites that journalism organizations host. Convergent journalists should be clear about the expectations of privacy that their online audience has. In addition, journalists should understand the extent to which the terms of service agreements by companies such as Google, WordPress and Twitter may impact the users' privacy.

VIEW FROM A PRO

MICHAEL MORISY

Journalists should become familiar with the federal Freedom of Information Act (FOIA), the Government in the Sunshine Act and their own state laws regarding access to government records stored data and meetings. Journalists can access plenty of resources online, including guides published by the Reporters Committee for Freedom of the Press (www.rcfp.org) and open government advocacy organized by the National Freedom of Information Coalition (www.nfoic.org).

Another more recent foray into government access in the digital era is MuckRock (www.muckrock.com), founded in 2010 by Mitchell Kotler and Michael Morisy. MuckRock is an online tool that helps citizens and journalists make document and data retrieval requests from the government through online submission forms available to the public.

Figure 12.1
Michael Morisy.

Morisy said government records are amazing tools for any kind of reporting.

"They're really useful for getting data and giving a better understanding of how the city and state work, and now there are so many different databases available," he said. "The best journalism comes when you marry large data sets with personal reporting. For us, being able to request hundreds of data sets makes for the ability to tell big stories."

For example, when MuckRock did census reporting on drone regulations, the company filed about a hundred information requests across America. As Morisy said,

"We are able to break news from Seattle to Maine and everywhere in between," Morisy said. "We're able to break local stories while telling the national story because we have the technology to manage this information. It's not super-impressive or cutting-edge technology. Just having a simple Google doc where people can collaborate can lead to great journalism."

Morisy, who covers startups and innovation at The Boston Globe in what he calls his "day job," helps to manage a small staff that has made more than 2,000 records requests since MuckRock launched. As an investigative reporter who has years of experience negotiating access to government records and data sets, Morisy offered several tips for convergent journalists:

- Make sure your request gets to the right person in the right office. "Often, someone complains that an agency is stonewalling, but it turns out the person emailed the wrong person or the message got caught by spam folder," Morisy said. "Follow up, let them know you're serious and set an expectation of when you expect a response. Make sure you're starting a conversation. Be very firm, but understand that this is a negotiation."

- Reach out to your state and local Freedom of Information advocacy groups to get a better grasp of the law in your area and know the avenues for administrative appeal of denials. "A lot of times, people get a road block or a rejection, and that's the end, they say, 'I can't afford a lawyer.' But lots of states have appeals processes. That means really knowing your rights and doing your homework," Morisy said. "Know what your rights are and what the exemptions are so you have the knowledge to push back. There are a lot of people who care about these issues. If you tap into that community, it's empowering."
- Name and shame agencies that don't follow the law. "Not every agency responds in the same way, so we've kind of seen it all over, but letting agencies know that you are willing to write about this and not let them ignore you really works," Morisy said, noting that MuckRock lists the requests it makes, how long they have been pending and which agencies are not in compliance. "Let them know you're serious about this. . . . Name-and-shame is a very powerful force, one that's not used enough."
- Make the records available to the public for more thorough and transparent reporting. "To me, one of the most exciting things today is that you can take information and share it with a knowledgeable audience," Morisy said. "One of the things we like to do at MuckRock is to get a big dataset, do a story from it, tell how we got it and then give it to you to see what you can do with it. That can make a better, more transparent story."

Copyright

Under federal law, when a person creates a new work – text, photograph, video, audio, even architecture, design, choreography and sculptures – a copyright automatically attaches to the work. This copyright gives authors of these works the right to control copying, sale, distribution and other uses of their works for "a limited time," according to Article I, Chapter 8 of the U.S. Constitution. Congress has extended that time to the life of the author plus 70 years, meaning that copyright protects most works created in the 20th century.

As such, convergent journalists should treat any work they come across that is not their own original creation with caution. While the Internet has made copying text, photos, music and video easier than ever, these works still carry copyright protection for their owners. Unauthorized use of these can lead to serious money damages. In 2013, photographer Daniel Morel was awarded $1.2 million in damages after a jury found that Getty Images and Agence France-Presse willfully used photos he took of an earthquake in Haiti and shared on Twitter. The fact that another Twitter user copied the photos and sold them to Getty and Agence France-Presse as if they were his own did not absolve the news agencies of liability for copyright infringement.

In short, just because you find something freely distributed on the Web does not mean you are free to use those items for your own journalistic purposes. So before you insert music behind a video you create or pull a photo from Flickr or Instagram to embed on your site, you should seek permission to use them or consider whether your use may be considered fair use.

The following section provides some guidance to make sure you use the works of others as safely as possible, particularly when you are unable to obtain permission from the creators of those works.

What does copyright not protect?

As mentioned above, copyright law protects original works of authorship, regardless of the medium in which they were created. This only protects works, but not facts, thoughts or ideas. You may safely report what you see with your own eyes, hear with your own ears or capture through your own lens. You may also repeat facts others have reported, as long as you use your own words to describe them. It's the words and photos and videos themselves – the tangible expression of those facts and events – that copyright law protects.

Also, certain kinds of works are not copyrightable. Publications of the federal government – including federal laws and regulations, U.S. Supreme Court and other federal court opinions and official investigations such as the 9/11 Commission Report – are not copyrightable and may be used and shared in full without permission. Recipes and lists of ingredients are not copyrightable, though the words people use to tell you how to prepare a meal may be. Short phrases, slogans and names are also not copyrightable, though they may be eligible for trademark protection. Trademark issues are not typically problematic for journalists because of the broad, fair-use protection for news uses in trademark law.

Works in the public domain – either because copyright protection was never sought or because the copyright has expired – are not copyrightable and may be used without permission. Unfortunately, because of the extension of copyright terms both in the United States and overseas, the public domain is becoming less of a meaningful option. In 2012, the Supreme Court in Golan vs. Holder allowed some foreign works previously in the public domain to fall back under copyright protection as authorized by the United States' treaties with other countries. This pulled the works of famed 20th century Russian composer Sergei Prokofiev, who died in 1953, out of the public domain. As a result, community orchestras that frequently perform "Peter and the Wolf", now need a license before putting on this popular piece for children.

Infringement

Copyright holders have several exclusive rights in their works, including the right to make copies, to distribute or sell copies, to permit or create derivative works such as writing a sequel and to perform or display the work publicly.

Without a license or permission, you may be infringing upon these exclusive rights when you try to use them, even for news purposes. Under federal law, copyright holders can seek civil damages against you. In 2014, minimum statutory damages were set at $750 per infringing use, with statutory damages of up to $30,000 per infringing use. That means that if you are found to be infringing on someone's copyright, he or she can seek, at a minimum, $750 in damages from you. If the infringement is found to be "willful" – that is, if you knew it was wrong and you did it anyway – the damages go up to a maximum of $150,000 per use. As was the case with Getty Images and Agence France-Presse for their unlawful use of Morel's photographs, damages for willful infringement can obviously escalate quickly.

Fair use

Fortunately for convergent journalists, fair use protects some uses of copyrighted works when done for news purposes. Unfortunately, it does not provide blanket protection, and there is a lot of grey area in how it applies. Fair use is enshrined in copyright law to reflect the founders' intentions in the Constitution that copyright be established "to promote the Progress of Science and Useful Arts." The defense allows some use of original works without permission, as long as those secondary uses are done for certain reasons. News purposes, educational purposes, commentary, research and scholarship are some of the reasons outlined in the Copyright Act.

Courts consider four factors in determining whether a secondary use of an original work is "fair" and thus can be done without permission or license from the copyright holder. These four factors are:

1   The purpose of the new use: Is it for profit? If so, as is the case for most news uses, courts are less likely to find fair use. Courts are friendlier on this point if the secondary work is "transformative," essentially creating something new from something old.

2   The nature of the original work: Is it fictional or fanciful? If so, as is the case for music and art including most photographs, courts are less favorable toward the fair-use argument. Original works that are more factual, historical or descriptive in nature – such as news articles, biographies and mug shots – make for better fair-use arguments.

3   The amount and substantiality of the use: How much of the original work is used, and how much of the secondary work does it comprise? A direct quote or a brief passage pulled from another news story is more likely to be fair use than an entire chapter of a book. Similarly, a few seconds of a two-minute video are more likely to be fair use than using the entire clip. This makes it difficult to claim fair use of photographs, which typically must be used in full to be meaningful; courts generally don't count cropping or editing of photos as reducing the "amount and substantiality" of their secondary use.

4   Harm to the market of the original: Did the secondary use somehow hurt the ability of the author to profit from the work? This includes taking a work that an author could license – such as a photograph or a song – and using it without permission or without paying for the license. Truly transformative works typically create a second market that doesn't harm the first. In one famous example, the Supreme Court ruled in Campbell vs. Acuff-Rose Music (1994) that the controversial rap group 2 Live Crew's version of "Pretty Woman", an indelicate parody of the original hit song "Oh, Pretty Woman" performed by Roy Orbison, was transformative and, if anything, it enhanced rather than detracted from the market for Orbison's version of the song.

215

CAUTIONARY TALE ON FAIR USE: HARPER & ROW VS. NATION ENTERPRISES (1985)

How much is too much, when it comes to using words from someone else's original work? Consider the case of former President Gerald Ford's memoirs.

In 1979, someone obtained the soon-to-be-published manuscript and leaked it to The Nation magazine. Ford had contracted to publish an excerpt in Time magazine, for which he received a $12,500 advance, with an additional $12,500 to be paid after the excerpt was published.

Before the excerpt was published, The Nation ran a 2,250-word story on the memoirs that included 300 words of direct quotes from the manuscript. This mostly focused on the most anticipated details of Ford's memoirs – his decision to pardon disgraced former president, Richard Nixon.

Time cancelled its deal with Ford and declined to pay the additional $12,500 to publish the excerpt; the publisher of Ford's memoirs, Harper & Row, filed a copyright infringement lawsuit against The Nation.

The dispute ultimately reached the U.S. Supreme Court. The Nation argued that its article was done for news purposes, that it was based on factual rather than fictional works and that it only used about 300 words from a 655-page manuscript – which should tilt the first three factors of the fair-use analysis in its favor.

The Supreme Court disagreed, ruling in 1985 that this was still copyright infringement. The harm to the market for the original – both in the cancellation of the Time deal and in taking away the original publisher's ability to control and profit from the first publication – turned out to be the most important factor in this case. Also, the court found that even though only 300 words were used, those words were the "heart of the book," enough to weigh against a finding of fair use.

Fair-use law is constantly shifting and developing, so relying on it as a defense is risky. In 2013, the Program on Information Justice and Intellectual Property at Washington College of Law and the Center for Social Media at American University created detailed guidelines for using original works in news reporting in the "Set of Principles in Fair Use for Journalism," available at www.pijip-impact.org.

Some federal district courts appear to be more open to finding fair use when the secondary work is not for profit and acknowledges the original work. In 2011, a federal district court in Nevada found that a not-for-profit organization in Oregon qualified for fair use, even though the organization posted an entire 33-paragraph article from the Las Vegas Review-Journal on its website (Righthaven vs. Jama). In another 2011 case, the same court found that copying eight full sentences on a realtor's blog was fair use because the sentences were largely factual, even if the blog had commercial purposes (Righthaven vs. Realty One Group).

These cases reflect a shifting understanding of fair use of news articles on the Web. However, you should not use long passages from other sources lightly. Remember that "fair use" only means you have the right to hire a lawyer to defend yourself against a copyright action, which can get expensive – even if you win.

So, it is wise to limit your borrowing of passages to the most essential information. Use one or two sentences and attribute to the original source by name, providing a hyperlink to the original if possible. Attribution and hyperlinking are evidence that you are acting in good faith, which will help you if you ever wind up in court.

The best practice is always to ask permission. Find the creator of the work you wish to use, particularly if it is visual or musical, and get permission in writing to use the work for the limited purpose you intend. Otherwise, consider options such as public domain works, works available for public use through copyright alternatives such as a Creative Commons license (creativecommons.org), or purchasing licenses through a subscription or wire service.

FINAL FOUR

If you take nothing else away from this chapter, here are four things you should remember:

1 When it comes to liability, publishing on the Web is the same as publishing in print or broadcast. You are responsible for any harm caused by what you publish, even if you are repeating what another publication said or what a source told you. While the Communications Decency Act protects hosting comments sections or sharing the words of others in digital spaces, anything else you publish opens you up to damages for defamation.

2 You have a right to photograph things happening in public places. In general, the First Amendment protects video and audio recording of matters of public interest – such as police behavior – occurring in public. However, several states require you to obtain the consent of the person being recorded, and you may be violating that person's privacy if you record a conversation or public act without his or her knowledge. Be aware of the rules in your area.

3 Open records laws such as the federal Freedom of Information Act are important tools that allow citizens access to government documents. Journalists often use these laws to tell important stories about how our elected officials do the public's business. Become familiar with your state's open records laws, particularly regarding how they apply to digital records such as databases.

4 Just because you find something on the Web for free doesn't mean you have a right to use it for journalism purposes. Photographs, video and music are subject to copyright law, which means that the creator of those works has an exclusive right to allow other uses. Seek permission to use the works of others. Also, understand that while the fair-use doctrine may allow some uses for news purposes, it does have limits. It is best to hyperlink to the original work when possible and to give credit to its author or creator.

Ethics in the Digital Age

Tracy Everbach

Introduction

Elizabeth Bassett was a junior at Texas Christian University when she found herself covering one of the most controversial stories of the year. Bassett had been assigned the religion beat on the student newspaper, the TCU Daily Skiff, for the semester. One day in January 2004, she received an anonymous message on her phone.

The tipster suggested she attend a meeting that night because "a professor has been unfairly discriminated against." Ever the curious journalist, Bassett went to the meeting. She found herself in the middle of a story about sexuality, the Christian Church and allegations of prejudice. The professor in question worked at the university's Brite Divinity School, affiliated with the Disciples of Christ Church. He said he had been barred from interviewing certain church ordination candidates because he was homosexual.

"I was three weeks into the semester and I had never written anything with this kind of importance," Bassett said. She sought advice from her editors at the student newspaper and the student publications director before she contacted sources and put together a story about the professor. On Jan. 28, 2004, her story ran at the top of the Skiff's front page with the headline, "Brite rep accuses Disciples' group of bigotry." It was the talk of campus that day.

Of course, that wasn't the end of the story. Bassett was assigned to cover her beat for the rest of the semester. The story was hers until May. Looking for a follow-up, she decided to find out more about the Disciples of Christ. She went to the campus church to talk to someone who could tell her more.

Inside the church, "a woman asked me where I was going," Bassett recalled. "I told her I wanted to learn more about the Disciples of Christ, but I didn't tell her I was a reporter." Bassett had been told in classes to always identify herself as a reporter, but she did not realize that she needed to represent herself as a journalist with every person she spoke to while on assignment. When she finally met with a pastor, Bassett told her that she was a student reporter and wanted to discuss homosexuality and the church. The pastor helped her with information, but she called the newspaper later to complain that Bassett had initially misrepresented herself.

"I sent her an email apologizing, saying I should have identified myself walking in," Bassett said. "She sent a very nice email back, saying, 'I understand you are learning,' and at the end she said, 'I understand this is a big story and it needs to be covered.'"

Bassett kept digging and found out from court records that the professor had been accused of sexual misconduct with a student. That led her to a court hearing in February. The story took more twists and turns and at every stage, Bassett had to make ethical decisions. She knew that what the paper printed could hurt the professor's reputation, the church's stake in the community and TCU's image, but her duty as a journalist was to find and report the truth. Her editors and advisers helped her along the way to ensure she treated her sources fairly and reported the story accurately. Ultimately, the professor resigned his position with the Disciples of Christ Church, but he kept his job teaching in the divinity school.

Bassett's experience demonstrates that ethics are a constant journalistic challenge. You may face these on a daily basis when working as a reporter, editor, producer, photojournalist or in any other journalism job. It is important to be armed with a code of ethics that can help guide you through decisions.

This chapter will explore the issues associated with ethical concerns that journalists encounter. It will also examine various codes of ethics, ethical dilemmas journalists often face and the overall value of ethics within the field of journalism.

220

Ethical Codes

Many reputable news organizations, such as the Chicago Tribune, Fort Worth Star-Telegram, Gannett Company, Los Angeles Times, National Public Radio, ProPublica and BusinessWeek, have their own ethics guidelines or handbooks. If you work for a news organization, you must familiarize yourself with its ethics policies.

The Society of Professional Journalists' Code of Ethics is considered a standard for the profession. The basic principles are:

1 Seek the truth and report it, by being honest, fair and courageous;
2 Minimize harm to sources, subjects and colleagues;
3 Act independently – meaning, recognizing that a journalist's first obligation is to the public and its right to know;
4 Be accountable to readers, viewers, listeners and other journalists.

(A copy of the SPJ Code of Ethics can be found here: www.spj.org/ethicscode.asp)

Seeking the truth and reporting it

Journalists have the power to help shape public opinion. Bill Kovach and Tom Rosenstiel write in their book, "The Elements of Journalism", that journalists' "first obligation is the truth." It goes without saying that journalists never should publish information that they know – or even suspect – is inaccurate. Fact checking is a foundation of journalism.

Journalists should go directly to sources for information, including people, documents, reports, legitimate websites and other factual elements. According to the Society of Professional Journalists' code, "deliberate distortion is never permissible," including text, quotes, still or video photography, maps, graphics or any other materials. Journalists always should check facts with more than one source to find "the best obtainable version of the truth," as Pulitzer Prize-winning journalist Carl Bernstein calls it.

It is more important than ever for journalists to uphold ethical and accurate reporting. The current media climate offers an infinite amount of information on the Internet, and readers and viewers are often confused about which sources are reliable. In a December 2013 Gallup poll, newspaper reporters and TV reporters ranked slightly above lawyers and slightly below local politicians in terms of the public's view on honesty and ethical standards. Only 21 percent of those polled said newspaper reporters had very high or high ethical standards, and 20 percent said the same of TV reporters. (The Gallup poll can be found here: www.gallup.com/poll/166298/honesty-ethics-rating-clergy-slides-new-low.aspx)

People mistrust journalists for a number of reasons. Sensationalism, celebrity news, talking heads, partisan reporting and some high-profile errors have contributed to the lack of public faith in the media. The shift of the industry from newspapers, magazines, television and radio to the Internet has caused a disruption that has forced many news organizations to seek new ways to attract audiences. Some strategies have worked and others have not.

For example, social media can be an excellent tool for journalists to share information with the public. Twitter, Facebook, Instagram, Reddit and other social media sites provide easy avenues to get important information to audiences that might not otherwise receive it. However, social media sites are also littered with misinformation. Social media and the Internet also have heightened journalists' and journalism organizations' desire to be "first," which has led to some embarrassing inaccuracies.

In January 2011, several major news organizations, including NPR, Reuters, CBS, Fox News and CNN, inaccurately tweeted that Rep. Gabrielle Giffords (D-Arizona) had died of gunshot wounds. In June 2012, both CNN and Fox News posted on their websites inaccurate stories about the U.S. Supreme Court ruling on the Affordable Care Act (ACA), featuring headlines that incorrectly said the court had struck down the mandate. In December 2012, several news outlets mistakenly named the brother of Adam Lanza as the person who had shot and killed 26 people and himself at Sandy Hook Elementary School in Newtown, Conneticut.

When bombs exploded at the April 2013 Boston Marathon, CNN, the Associated Press, Fox News and even The Boston Herald reported arrests when none had happened. The New York Post printed on its tabloid cover the photos of two men who never were charged with anything, under the headline "Bag Men." (The men later sued for libel.) All of these media organizations quickly corrected their errors, but they damaged their reputations and endured intense criticism.

Journalists can remedy negative public perceptions by espousing accuracy, transparency and fairness. Anonymous sources should only be used under extreme circumstances, when the information cannot be obtained any other way. "The public is entitled to as much information as possible on sources' reliability," SPJ's Code of Ethics says. In the errors with Giffords, Lanza, the ACA and the Boston bombers, sources were absent and the headlines were inaccurate, leading to an erosion of public trust.

Journalists should always explain how they got their information. The public deserves to know the sources of the information it is receiving. Also, anyone accused of wrongdoing should have the chance to respond.

VERIFY, VERIFY, VERIFY

Accuracy is paramount to journalists' and news organizations' credibility. Having a verification system in place can protect reporters from making errors. Some simple rules for accuracy and truthfulness are:

- When in doubt, check it out. Verify everything with more than one source, including names, titles, places, addresses, numbers, percentages, links and other factual information. A simple factual error can taint an entire story.

- Never assume. Journalists who make errors often do so because they made an assumption about something that was incorrect. Always ask questions. Double check and triple check everything, including spelling and grammar.

- Never speculate. Only publish what you know is true and can back up with documentation and/or sources. Taking a risk with speculation is likely to damage a journalist's credibility and that of the news organization.

- Never fabricate. It goes without saying that making up information is a major ethical breach.

- Never plagiarize. Plagiarism is stealing. In the Internet age especially, taking information from another source is easy to trace.

Minimizing harm

An aspect of the job many journalists find difficult is talking to victims and their families. Often these sources are in distress, so interviewing them can be challenging. Mark Poepsel learned this lesson when he was a television reporter in the Quad Cities area on the Iowa-Illinois border. Poepsel was 22 and had recently graduated from college when he and a photographer covered a story about a man who had been struck and killed by a car.

The man lived in a rural area and had been picking up his mail at a mailbox when he was hit. Before Poepsel left on the assignment, his assigning editor discovered that one of the man's grandchildren had also been killed within weeks of the accident.

"It got to be a bigger story because there had been another death covered in local media," Poepsel said.

When he and the cameraman arrived at the scene, they began photographing blood on the highway where the man was killed. Suddenly, the victim's daughter appeared and began yelling at them, accusing the journalists of making a profit from the family's misery.

Poepsel apologized to the woman and promised the footage of the blood would not air.

"I told her I didn't enjoy doing stories like this," he said. Poepsel didn't use the graphic images he promised not to use.

When he got back to the newsroom, he called one of his former journalism professors from the University of Missouri-Columbia and asked why journalists needed to cover stories like this.

The professor told him, "Because he (the man) was important to your community."

Making ethical decisions in difficult situations is often painful. Most things like this happen to people who are not public figures and are not accustomed to talking to reporters. On top of that, family members are often in shock and suffering emotional pain. Reporters and photographers must weigh the public's right to know information with the harm they may cause to relatives, friends and others who know the victim.

The SPJ Code of Ethics advises journalists to show compassion and sensitivity toward victims. Explain clearly that you are working on a story and that you would like to talk to them about their situation. If these people do not want to talk or are overcome with grief, ask if someone else may speak on their behalf. Reporters should also keep in mind that private people have a right to privacy if they ask for it.

VIEW FROM A PRO

MATTHEW LAPLANTE

Reporter Matthew LaPlante faced the most challenging ethical decisions of his career when he and a photojournalist traveled to Ethiopia in 2011 to report on infanticide in some tribal communities.

He and photographer Rick Egan wanted to find out more about *mingi*, a superstition that sometimes results in the killing of young children in southern Ethiopian tribes. LaPlante said,

"Children are determined to have the *mingi* curse for many reasons, but one common reason is that their top teeth came in before their bottom ones," LaPlante said. "When this happens the child will either be thrown to crocodiles, or they will be left in the bush, or suffocated with dirt."

Figure 13.1 *Matthew LaPlante.*
(COURTESY OF MATTHEW LAPLANTE/RICK EGAN)

As a former national security reporter for The Salt Lake Tribune who had traveled to Iraq, he was used to covering conflict and other cultures. He also had served as an intelligence analyst for the U.S. Navy.

But preparing for this trip was harrowing. The tribes lived in extremely remote locations that were inaccessible most of the year because of washed-out roads. The people who lived in the tribes had no exposure to media and didn't understand what journalists did. The languages they spoke were not easily translated. As LaPlante said,

"We had many ethical challenges," LaPlante said. "How do you put this in a cultural context without validating it, but without vilifying it? How do you explain the media to people who have never seen a newspaper, television or Internet, so they can make an intelligent decision on whether to speak to us?"

The journalists also faced a horrifying ethical issue: What would they do if a child were sacrificed when they were present?

"We ultimately decided we were there as journalists, observers, if that meant we were going to stand by and watch a child killed, that was our job and we would fulfill it," LaPlante said. "We also decided that if either of us couldn't do that, that neither of us would hold the other responsible, because our humanity came before the dedication to journalism."

Fortunately, they did not have to test their protocol. They did not witness any sacrifices when documenting the story.

Their story ran on CNN.com in November 2011. (The story may be found here: www.cnn.com/2011/11/05/world/africa/mingi-ethiopia/)

In 2012, LaPlante and Egan won the Ancil Payne Award for Ethics in Journalism for their "careful consideration of the ethical issues in advance," according to the judges.

LaPlante returned to Ethiopia one year after the reporting trip. He traveled with the same interpreter whom he and Egan had hired the previous year.

"He got a phone call," LaPlante said. "He pulled over and was crying. He told me, the tribe had decided to end *mingi*."

The Dart Center for Journalism and Trauma website (dartcenter. org) offers tips and support to journalists who cover victims of violence, helping them approach people with sensitivity and compassion. The tips include not only how to cover shootings, natural disasters, war and sexual violence, but also how to interview children. Journalists should take special precautions when interviewing children, who are often naïve about how media work. The Dart Center advises journalists to get parental consent before photographing or interviewing a child, to set ground rules about information on and off the record and not to make promises they cannot keep.

The right to privacy and the right to know

Even if information is publicly available, journalists must compare the individual's right to privacy with the public's right to know. Ethical decisions are often made after serious discussions among reporters, editors, photojournalists and producers. For instance, in January 2014, Grantland.com, a sports and popular culture website, published an apology for a story it ran on the inventor of a golf putter. The original story, following a trail of public records about the inventor, revealed she was a transgender person who lived as a woman but had once been a man. During Grantland's reporting, but before the story was published, she committed suicide. When Grantland.com ran the story, many readers protested, saying the "outing" was a privacy invasion. They also criticized the story, saying that the reporting may have contributed to her death since the reporter had "outed" her to an investor before the story was published.

On the other hand, reporters can consider public figures fair game for questions and public records searches. Their voluntary public status means they hold a certain level of public trust and are subject to more scrutiny than private figures. When it was revealed that President Bill Clinton had a romantic relationship with White House intern Monica Lewinsky while in office, the media covered the story closely. The relationship became the subject of a federal investigation and media outlets published the results as well as the sexual details.

AN ETHICS CHECK LIST

Each ethical decision is different. Every case ideally should be considered not only by the reporter, but also by other decision-makers in the news organization. Most ethical decisions are group decisions made after thoughtful discussion.

Bob Steele of the Poynter Institute, a school for journalists, recommends that journalists should ask the following questions to make good ethical decisions:

- What do I know? What do I need to know?
- What is my journalistic purpose?
- What are my ethical concerns?
- What organizational policies and professional guidelines should I follow?
- How can I include other people, with different perspectives and diverse ideas, in the decision-making process?
- Who are the stakeholders – those affected by my decision? What are their motivations? Which are legitimate?
- What if the roles were reversed? How would I feel if I were in the shoes of one of the stakeholders?
- What are the possible consequences of my actions? Short term? Long term?
- What are my alternatives to maximize my truth-telling responsibility and minimize harm?
- Can I clearly and fully justify my thinking and my decision? To my colleagues? To the stakeholders? To the public?

(A link to Steele's article about the ethical questions can be found here: www.poynter.org/latest-news/everyday-ethics/talk-about-ethics/1750/ask-these-10-questions-to-make-good-ethical-decisions/)

Independence

One of the most important tenets of American journalism is journalists' independence from outside influence. To maintain autonomy, journalists should not take directions from advertisers or other financial supporters of their media organizations. They also shouldn't take gifts, bribes, junkets or other monetary or material rewards in exchange for their work. They do not compensate sources for information or interviews.

Journalists should be neutral observers, not advocates or opponents of the issues they cover. (The notable exception is critics, reviewers and opinion writers, whose work should clearly be labeled opinion.) For this reason, journalists do not join political campaigns, donate to candidates or associate themselves with causes that may create the appearance they are biased. Sports journalists, in particular, should not root for the teams they cover or take sides in competitions.

Former sports writer Steve Fox found himself in an uncomfortable position in 1995 when he covered the Preakness Stakes at Pimlico Race Course in Baltimore. He walked into the press box and facing him were three betting windows set up for the sports writers.

"I asked one or two people, 'Is this a regular thing at press boxes at horse tracks?' And they just seemed to shrug," he said. "My recollection was being in awe of the writers going up there and betting. It didn't even cross my mind to bet; it seemed one of those clear-cut issues."

Fox, now a journalism professor at the University of Massachusetts-Amherst, said he teaches his students that sports journalists are not "fan-boys and fan-girls. They have to cover the good, the bad and the ugly. There is a lot going on that you will have to report that does not portray your team well."

To avoid conflicts of interest, journalists should not make their friends into sources or their sources into friends. If they find themselves in a romantic relationship with a source, they must disclose it to their superiors. As far as social media friendships, always check with your organization's policies on whom and how you can "friend," follow or retweet.

Accountability

Journalists and journalism organizations must be accountable to their audiences. This means they should listen to audience members' complaints and grievances. Most newspapers list factual corrections on a daily basis, from minor mistakes such as misspellings to more egregious infractions like reporting a death that did not occur or accusing the wrong suspect in a crime. News organizations publish letters to the editor, op-ed commentary and other forms of public feedback.

With the advent of the Internet, news organizations began offering online comments sections to their audiences. By the end of the first decade of the 21st century, many forums also attracted harassers, haters and Internet trolls. Some news organizations, such as the Christian Science Monitor, removed comments from most stories because of abusive, uncivil and offensive commenters. The New York Times monitors comments, only posting the ones it selects. Many other news organizations adjust policies to require commenters to sign in with their names or social media profiles, disallowing anonymous comments so that those who post are accountable.

Journalists should explain the methods and motives behind their reporting. In most cases, they must identify themselves as journalists. The SPJ Code of Ethics states that journalists should not go undercover to get information unless it cannot be obtained any other way. If journalists must misrepresent themselves to get a story, they should disclose the methods they used.

In the 1990s, ABC News found out the hard way that such investigations could prove detrimental. The organization sent journalists undercover to get jobs at Food Lion supermarkets in North and South Carolina. The plan was to investigate practices behind the scenes with hidden cameras. ABC News later aired a report on its show PrimeTime Live, alleging unsafe and unsanitary practices in the meat department. These included "selling old meat that was washed with bleach to kill odor, selling cheese that had been gnawed by rats and working off the time clock," according to Kristen Rasmussen of the Reporters Committee for Freedom of the Press, a nonprofit organization that provides legal assistance to journalists.

Food Lion then sued ABC, charging illegal reporting methods. The court eventually ruled that ABC committed fraud because the producers had lied on their Food Lion job applications, failing to disclose they were journalists. An appeals court later ruled the producers had trespassed because they did not have permission to record anything on the stores' premises. (An account of the case by the Reporters Committee for Freedom of the Press may be found here:

www.rcfp.org/browse-media-law-resources/news-media-law/news-media-and-law-spring-2012/landmark-food-lion-case)

The precedent set for journalists was that truth is not always a defense, especially if the methods used to discover the truth violate the law. Undercover and hidden-camera investigations, which had become popular media tools in the 1990s, decreased drastically.

Voice to the Voiceless

One of the most compelling duties of a journalist is to give voice to the voiceless – to be mindful of those who do not have power and influence in society and pay attention to their concerns. While official sources usually are easiest to reach, all members of a community have important voices. Seeking out those who do not have the ear of the media will almost always make a story more complete and compelling.

Academic analyses of media content have repeatedly shown that news media tend to disproportionately focus on white male sources and under-represent women and people of color. Studies show that people of color are often misrepresented as primary suspects in crimes, athletes or entertainers. Such stereotypes persist in the coverage of women as well. For example, the coverage of women political candidates often dwells on their appearance and family lives rather than their platforms or issues of concern. Journalists are advised in the SPJ Code of Ethics to "avoid stereotyping by race, gender, age, religion, ethnicity, geography, sexual orientation, disability, physical appearance or social status."

Because many newsrooms lack racial and ethnic diversity, journalists must be mindful of all members of their communities. The American Society of News Editors (ASNE) takes an annual census of newspaper newsrooms; in 2013 it showed that only 12 percent of employees nationwide were non-white, while 37 percent of the U.S. population is made up of people of color. ASNE also reported that two-thirds of newsroom employees are male. (The full ASNE report may be found here: http://asne.org/content.asp?pl=121&sl=284&contentid=284)

The Radio Television Digital News Association (RTDNA), which represents broadcasters, reported that in 2013 people of color made up 21 percent of television news employees and 11 percent of radio news employees. Women made up 40 percent of the television news workers and 34 percent of radio news workers. In all cases, women and people of color were less likely to be editors, general managers

230

and news directors than white males. (The entire RTDNA information may be found here: www.rtdna.org/article/little_change_for_women_minorities_in_tv_radio#.Uu64vP3nVfN)

All journalists are able to report on various communities, but people with different backgrounds can improve the overall understanding of various cultures. For this reason and others, SPJ's code advises journalists to "examine their own cultural values and avoid imposing them on others." Putting oneself in another's shoes is a skill that requires empathy and thought. Reaching out to diverse sources will not only make a story more complete, but will also better serve the audience.

One example of media stereotyping is demonstrated in two photos that were released during Hurricane Katrina in 2005 and published on Yahoo! News. One, circulated by the Associated Press, showed a young, black man wading through the water, carrying a case of soda and pulling a black garbage bag. The caption on the photo of the black man reads, "A young man walks through chest deep water after looting a grocery store in New Orleans on Tuesday, August 30, 2005."

The other photo, distributed by Agence France-Press, shows a young, white man and young, white woman walking in the water. The woman is carrying food packages. The caption for the photo of the white couple reads, "Two residents wade through chest-deep water after finding bread and soda from a local grocery store after Hurricane Katrina came through the area in New Orleans, Louisiana."

Many people who circulated the photos on the Internet charged that racial bias caused journalists to label the black man a looter, while stating that the white people found their food. The Associated Press later confirmed that its photographer witnessed the black man taking items from a store. Agence France-Press' photographer did not see where the white people obtained their goods. (The photos may be found here: www.flagarts.com/faculty-staff/Jennifer%20Spensieri/documents/HurricaneKatrina.pdf)

The photos and their captions show that journalists must take care with the words they use to describe people in order to avoid stereotyping or other misperceptions. They must look beyond their own biases to report fairly.

231

FINAL FOUR

If you take nothing else away from this chapter, here are four things you should remember:

1 Journalists are charged with upholding accuracy and truth. To maintain the trust of the public, journalists must verify all information they report. They must never distort information or report false information. They also should not judge the subjects of their stories. They should avoid stereotypes and strive for diversity in the sources and subjects they cover.

2 Journalists are obligated to minimize harm. Often this means weighing the public's right to know with an individual's right to privacy. Journalists must be compassionate and empathetic. They should also be fearless about holding those in power responsible for their actions.

3 Journalists must maintain their independence and autonomy. Journalists do not accept money, gifts, trips or favors in exchange for information. They do not take orders from advertisers or financial backers. They are not participants, advocates or critics. They are independent observers.

4 Journalists should be accountable to their audiences and their sources. They should correct errors, never misrepresent themselves, use anonymous sources only when the information cannot be obtained elsewhere and avoid going undercover. They should be transparent about the methods and sources they use. Journalists' first obligation is to their readers, viewers or listeners.

About the Authors

Bob Britten is an assistant professor at West Virginia University's Reed College of Media, where he teaches visual journalism. He has worked as a reporter, graphics reporter, designer, art director, graphics editor and editorial director, for newspapers and magazines including the Greenville Record-Argus, Meadville Tribune, Columbia Missourian, Seattle Times, Allegheny magazine, and Farm Journal (as well as its subsidiary, Beef Today). Britten has taught courses in media design, information graphics, data visualization, interactive design and visual literacy. He also researches visual communication, rhetoric and culture, especially the role of these in building and maintaining social memory. He earned his bachelor's degree from Allegheny College and earned his master's and Ph.D. from the University of Missouri.

Steven Chappell is an instructor of mass media and director of student publications at Northwest Missouri State University. He is also the founder of the Twitter feed @comminternships and its companion blog, www.comminternships.com, which shares internship and entry-level openings in communication jobs around the globe. Chappell has been a professional journalist for more than 30 years and a college media adviser for 20 years. He was named to the College Media Advisers Four-Year College Newspaper Adviser Honor Roll in 2004 for outstanding media advising and his service to the organization. His Twitter feed has landed him roles as a communications internship expert with organizations such as ProfNet, Reuters and LinkedIn.

Erika Engstrom is a professor of communication studies at the University of Nevada, Las Vegas. She has worked as a radio news reporter, anchor, producer and television news writer and production assistant in various markets. She has published several books, including "Mad Men and Working Women" (with Tracy Lucht, Jane Marcellus and Kimberly Wilmot Voss), "Television, Religion and Supernatural" (with Joseph M. Valenzano III) and "The Bride Factory". She earned her bachelor's and master's degrees from the University of Central Florida and her Ph.D. in mass communication from the University of Florida.

Tracy Everbach is an associate professor in the Mayborn School of Journalism at the University of North Texas. She teaches writing and reporting; race, gender and media; and graduate classes on qualitative research and media theories. Her research interests concentrate on media diversity, including gender and race in newsroom management and media coverage. She earned a Ph.D. in journalism from the University of Missouri in 2004, a master's degree in journalism from the University of Texas at Austin in 2000 and a bachelor's degree in journalism from Boston University in 1984. She worked as a newspaper reporter for 14 years, 12 on the Metro desk of The Dallas Morning News and two at The Boston Herald.

Vincent F. Filak is an associate professor at the University of Wisconsin Oshkosh, where he teaches writing and editing courses and serves as the adviser to the school's award-winning newspaper, The Advance-Titan. He has taught journalism courses at the University of Missouri, the University of Wisconsin and Ball State University, where he also advised the Ball State Daily News. He produced the earlier version of this book, "Convergent Journalism: An Introduction", with Dr. Stephen Quinn and co-authored the book, "The Journalist's Handbook for Online Editing", with Dr. Kenneth L. Rosenauer. He has contributed to the books "Media in an American Crisis: Studies of Sept. 11, 2001" and "Understanding Media Convergence" and has extensively published research on issues of media convergence, e-learning and student journalism.

Jennifer George-Palilonis is the George & Francis Ball Distinguished Professor of Multimedia at Ball State University. There, she directs the nationally recognized Journalism Graphics sequence and teaches upper level courses in information graphics reporting, interaction design and multimedia storytelling. Her research focuses on active reading in digital environments, interaction design, information visualization, human-computer interaction and multimedia storytelling. In 2013, George-Palilonis was named the national Journalism and Mass Communication Teacher of the Year by the Scripps Howard Foundation.

Timothy R. Gleason is a professor of journalism at the University of Wisconsin Oshkosh. He was previously a newspaper photojournalist and an associate producer of a public television news program for children in Ohio. Gleason earned a bachelor's degree in Studio Art from SUNY Brockport; a master's degree in journalism from Ohio State University; and a doctorate in communication studies (cognates in American culture studies and qualitative/historical methods) from Bowling Green State University. He has worked as a newspaper photojournalist and won three Ohio Associated Press awards.

Sara Steffes Hansen is an assistant professor in the department of journalism at the University of Wisconsin Oshkosh. She teaches advertising, public relations and new media courses for the department of journalism and the college of business' Interactive Web Management degree. Her research focuses on strategic communication in interactive media, with emphasis on consumer engagement with marketing campaigns via social media. Her research has appeared in several journals and books, including Journal of Marketing Communications, Journal of Interactive Advertising and Journal of Marketing Management. She earned her MBA at the University of Colorado-Denver. She previously worked as a manager, director and consultant in public relations and marketing for Fortune 500 and high-tech companies, including Kinder Morgan, Inc., CIBER, Inc. and J. D. Edwards (now part of Oracle Corp.). Her first job was as a news reporter and state news editor for the Marshfield News-Herald.

Glenn Hubbard is an assistant professor in the school of communication at East Carolina University. He previously taught at the University of Texas at Arlington, the University of Tennessee and Appalachian State University. His research has been published in the Journal of Broadcasting and Electronic Media, Journalism and Mass Communication Educator, Atlantic Journal of Communication and Journal of Radio and Audio Media. His primary research interest is in convergent journalism education, and he has also published articles on broadcast localism and the effects of media production elements on audience preferences. He is a former news anchor/reporter at WLW in Cincinnati. He previously worked for several media outlets in western North Carolina, both in radio and TV/video production. In addition, he is a musician, record producer and songwriter with credits on more than a dozen album releases. He earned his Ph.D. at the University of Tennessee and his master's and bachelor's degrees at Appalachian State University.

Gary Larson is an associate professor-in-residence at the University of Nevada, Las Vegas, where he serves as the undergraduate coordinator for the Hank Greenspun School of Journalism. He teaches courses in television production and broadcast journalism, including a student-produced news webcast program. He has extensive experience in the broadcast news industry and earned his Ph.D. from the University of Minnesota, his master's in mass communication from North Dakota State University and his bachelor's degree in anthropology from the University of Minnesota.

Scott Reinardy was a newspaper reporter and editor for 18 years before earning his Ph.D. at the University of Missouri. As an associate professor in the University of Kansas School of Journalism and Mass Communications, he is the News and Information Track chairman and teaches intermediate and advanced multimedia journalism courses. He has a master's degree in journalism from the University of Missouri and a bachelor's degree in journalism and history from South Dakota State University.

Daxton R. "Chip" Stewart is an associate professor in the Bob Schieffer College of Communication at Texas Christian University, where he has taught classes in media law and ethics since 2008 and has served as associate dean since 2013. He began his journalism career as a sportswriter in Dallas before attending law school at the University of Texas. After practicing law in Texas, he became a city editor on the cops and courts beat and a columnist at the Columbia Missourian while earning his master's and doctorate in journalism and Master of Laws in Dispute Resolution at the University of Missouri. He has published articles in journals such as Journalism and Mass Communication Quarterly, Communication Law and Policy, American Journalism, the Journal of Media Law and Ethics, the Journal on Telecommunications and High Technology Law, the Journal of Dispute Resolution and the Appalachian Journal of Law. He was editor of Dispute Resolution Magazine, the quarterly publication of the American Bar Association's Section on Dispute Resolution, from 2007 to 2012. He edited the book "Social Media and the Law: A Guidebook for Communication Students and Professionals" (Routledge, 2013).

Index

241

243